"For years I've tried to teach my church that fear is the dark room where negatives develop. If you are one of the millions who struggles with the debilitating symptoms of panic attacks or other anxiety disorders, let Lance's intimate, personal journey shed light on steps to overcoming and beating this crippling disorder. With candor and humor he offers practical tools that will help you step out of the darkness of fear and into the light of a confident life."

> —Ray Johnston
> Founding pastor, Bayside Church, Granite Bay, CA,
> Bestselling author of *The Hope Quotient*

"In *How to Live in Fear*, my dear friend Lance Hahn, with unbridled authenticity and transparency, confronts the reality of anxiety disorder and fear with the grace and compassion of Christ. Pastor Lance elevates the eternal truth that we are not defined by our weaknesses. We stand defined by God's strength."

> —Rev. Dr. Samuel Rodriguez
> Lead pastor, New Season Christian Worship Center,
> Sacramento, CA

"Lance Hahn has given us a transparent masterpiece on human fear. Both compelling and clinical, *How to Live in Fear* is even bigger in content than the title suggests. Lance's use of his own life story is risky, but it's a risk I'm glad he took. Not only did I learn, but so will the thousands of people I'm about to recommend this book to."

> —Scott Hagan
> Founding pastor, Real Life Church, Sacramento, CA

"Lance's book, *How to Live in Fear*, addresses how to detect and defeat anxiety and conquer fear. Lance honestly opens up his own journey while giving practical and spiritual principles that will break the pattern and launch you into a life of breakthroughs. I highly recommend this helpful book on living victoriously."

> —Sean Smith
> Author of *I Am Your Sign* and *Prophetic Evangelism*

"We all want fear to go away—far, far away. But as long as we are living and breathing in this world, rest assured, fear will come knocking. . . . Through the pages of his book, Lance gives us tangible action steps for when we feel paralyzed by fear. He doesn't preach to us or offer us religious jargon. Instead, he boldly shares his own battle with the demon of fear. Lance's transparency is an extreme act of courage rarely displayed by those who hold the position of pastor/church leader. I highly recommend this book."

—Jenny Williamson

Founder/CEO, Courage Worldwide, Inc.

"Jesus said 'Blessed are those who mourn, for they shall be comforted' (Matthew 5:4). If you have ever been stressed or depressed, then my friend Lance Hahn has written a book that will bring you comfort, hope, and peace. Lance is vulnerable, transparent, and compelling on every page. Get yourself some help and read this book!"

—Dr. John Jackson

President, William Jessup University

Speaker, consultant, and author

"There is a reason the most repeated commandment in all of Scripture is 'Do not fear.' Every one of us faces fear in some area of our lives . . . and yet it's something we rarely talk about. Lance Hahn, with authenticity that is so refreshing, has decided to talk about this issue. In *How to Live in Fear*, Lance invites the reader on a journey of walking with a loving Father and the insight and lessons he has learned along the way. There is great strength and courage to be found for others when someone opens up his life, and I am grateful Lance has done this."

—Banning Liebscher

Founder and pastor, Jesus Culture

"If you're living in fear, then you're probably tired of listening to theories from people who aren't. That's where you find a friend in Lance Hahn and his extremely practical book, *How to Live in Fear*, an honest and vulnerable guide providing you with the help you need to survive fear day to day . . . when it won't go away."

—Jonathan McKee

Author of *More Than Just the Talk* and *52 Ways to Connect with Your Smartphone Obsessed Kid*

"Real. That's what Lance is. Hope. That's what this book brings. Confidence. That's what I have, knowing you are about to engage the fear with a friend like Lance."

—Brad Franklin
Senior pastor, Lakeside Church, Folsom, CA

"Lance Hahn tackles this real-life problem—paralyzing fear and anxiety—with studied insight, disarming humor, and helpful strategies that are both biblical and practical. The crippling tendency to 'freak out' for no normal reason has been Lance's own lifelong struggle, and he describes it with a transparency that is both painful and hilarious. This book will be a welcome companion and counselor to the many who are paralyzed by this same condition or who love someone else who is."

—Kirk Bottomly
Senior pastor, Fair Oaks Presbyterian Church,
Fair Oaks, CA

"We would all rather go through our greatest struggles in private. Yet many pastors are not given that luxury. Lance had a nearly debilitating battle with anxiety in front of thousands. Consequently, he publically modeled perseverance, humility, and faith. Now, through this amazingly vulnerable and insightful book, How To Live in Fear, multitudes will find freedom as well."

—Francis Anfuso
Senior pastor, The Rock of Roseville, Roseville, CA

"It doesn't matter what background or context we come from—we have all struggled with fear. Personally, having been controlled by fear in various stages of my life, I can appreciate Lance's transparency and honesty in this book. His sincere and practical writing style makes it easy for anyone to benefit from his wisdom and insight for overcoming fear. If you're struggling with fear in your life, this book is for you."

—Alex Vaiz
Senior pastor, Vida Church, Sacramento, CA

"With great transparency, Lance Hahn shares how he has learned to live with the 'thorn in the flesh' called fear and to experience the sufficiency of God's grace in his life. If you know what it is to live in fear, you're not alone. This book will give you the hope you are looking for and the help you need to live a more peaceful, productive, and fulfilling life."

—Perry Kallevig
Pastor, Harvest Church, Elk Grove (Sacramento), CA

"We've had the privilege to walk closely beside Lance Hahn as a fellow pastor and friend in the community. His transparency, authenticity, and relentless commitment to the Word of God make him an irresistible person of influence for God."

—Don Proctor and Christa Proctor
Lead pastors, Impact Church, Roseville, CA
Founders, City Pastors Fellowship

"I had no idea this book would strike such a nerve, personally and among my friends. Honestly, I had a difficult time reading the book because everyone kept grabbing it off my desk. Through funny and embarrassing personal examples, Lance disarms and demystifies our hidden lives of fear and anxiety and delivers the steady, calming perspective of our Heavenly Father. "

—Ryan MacDiarmid
Lead pastor, Creekside Church, Rocklin, CA

How to Live in Fear

Mastering the Art of Freaking Out

Lance Hahn

W Publishing Group

An Imprint of Thomas Nelson

Published in Nashville, Tennessee, by W Publishing, an imprint of Thomas Nelson.

Author is represented by the literary agency of Alive Communications, Inc., 7680 Goddard Street, Suite 200, Colorado Springs, CO 80920, www.alivecommunications.com.

Thomas Nelson titles may be purchased in bulk for educational, business, fund-raising, or sales promotional use. For information, please e-mail SpecialMarkets@ThomasNelson.com.

Any Internet addresses, phone numbers, or company or product information printed in this book are offered as a resource and are not intended in any way to be or to imply an endorsement by Thomas Nelson, nor does Thomas Nelson vouch for the existence, content, or services of these sites, phone numbers, companies, or products beyond the life of this book.

Unless otherwise noted, Scripture quotations are taken from the esv˚ Bible (The Holy Bible, English Standard Version˚). Copyright © 2001 by Crossway, a publishing ministry of Good News Publishers. Used by permission. All rights reserved.

Scripture quotations marked cev are from the Contemporary English Version. Copyright © 1991, 1992, 1995 by American Bible Society. Used by permission.

Scripture quotations marked exb are from the Expanded Bible. Copyright © 2011 by Thomas Nelson. Used by permission. All rights reserved.

Scripture quotations marked the message are from The Message. Copyright © by Eugene H. Peterson 1993, 1994, 1995, 1996, 2000, 2001, 2002. Used by permission of Tyndale House Publishers, Inc.

Scripture quotations marked ncv are from the New Century Version˚. © 2005 by Thomas Nelson. Used by permission. All rights reserved.

Scripture quotations marked niv are from the Holy Bible, New International Version˚, niv˚. Copyright © 1973, 1978, 1984, 2011 by Biblica, Inc.˚ Used by permission of Zondervan. All rights reserved worldwide. www.zondervan.com. The "niv" and "New International Version" are trademarks registered in the United States Patent and Trademark Office by Biblica, Inc.˚

Scripture quotations marked nkjv are from the New King James Version˚. © 1982 by Thomas Nelson. Used by permission. All rights reserved.

Scripture quotations marked nlt are from the Holy Bible, New Living Translation. © 1996, 2004, 2007, 2013 by Tyndale House Foundation. Used by permission of Tyndale House Publishers, Inc., Carol Stream, Illinois 60188. All rights reserved.

Scripture quotations marked tlb are from The Living Bible. Copyright © 1971. Used by permission of Tyndale House Publishers, Inc., Carol Stream, Illinois 60188. All rights reserved.

Scripture quotations marked the voice are from The Voice™. © 2012 by Ecclesia Bible Society. Used by permission. All rights reserved. Note: Italics in quotations from The Voice are used to "indicate words not directly tied to the dynamic translation of the original language but that bring out the nuance of the original, assist in completing ideas, and . . . provide readers with information that would have been obvious to the original audience" (The Voice, preface).

ISBN 978-0-7180-3858-8 (eBook)

Library of Congress Cataloging-in-Publication Data

Hahn, Lance.
  How to live in fear: mastering the art of freaking out / Lance Hahn.
    pages cm
  ISBN 978-0-7180-3542-6 (trade paper)
  1. Fear—Religious aspects—Christianity. 2. Anxiety—Religious aspects—Christianity. 3. Christian life. I. Title.
  BV4908.5.H34 2016
  248.8'6—dc23

                                                        2015024758

Printed in the United States of America

16 17 18 19 20   RRD   10 9 8 7 6 5 4 3 2 1

To my beautiful and loving wife, Suzi, and my incredible daughters, Jillian and Andie: Thank you for sharing me with the world and being giving of your time with me so that others may be blessed. Thank you as well for your love and constant prayer for me.

To my mom, dad, brother, and sister: Thank you for loving me and guiding me in my struggle, and thank you for your patience as we figured this thing out.

To my Bridgeway Christian Church family: I love you all and am so thankful that you have allowed me to be transparent and authentic in my journey.

To my assistant and friend Joanne: You were a prayer warrior defending me when I was down. Your prayers and those of my intercessor team kept me standing when I should have fallen down.

To Robert Nolan, who put his heart and amazing writing skills to work for the kingdom and contributed to make this book what God intended.

CONTENTS

CONTENTS

FOREWORD

I am convinced the best place to find a classic sport coat is on the neglected clothing rack of a thrift store. On one particular afternoon I ventured into one of my favorite thrift stores, tucked away in a quiet corridor of the city, and found the perfect sport coat hanging in a dimly lit corner. The cashier was quick to tell me that it was a top find and a great deal.

As I left, I encountered a young lady who recognized me from church. I was taken with her openness and transparency as she poured out her heart to me. She described how God was doing wonderful things in her life and how her outlook had changed.

She further explained that her pastor, Lance Hahn, was the reason for her season of restoration, joy, and wholeness. She said, "I love his transparency and honesty." I soon realized I had come to the store not to find the perfect coat but to make a connection with a soul on a new and vibrant journey, thanks to my friend in ministry, Pastor Lance Hahn.

Transparency and honesty are two missing elements in conversations today. Don't get me wrong; people still love to talk. We talk all the time. And with the emergence of technological advances such as texting, e-mail, and social media, we can have conversations with just about anyone, anywhere, at any time. Yet there still seems to be a reluctance to open up and share the intimate details of the darker side of life. Our conversations seem superficial, centering on what projects the best image of ourselves.

The reality is that this is not reality. For anyone. Furthermore, the subject of mental health is often shunned or avoided when discussing faith and serving God. This absence of honest dialogue leads many to believe that they are alone in their battles. Rarely do we find a person willing to begin a compassionate conversation about mental illness that will help remove the stigma, the shame, and the shroud of silence associated with mental health struggles. Thankfully, this book presents one of those rare opportunities to sit down and have that very conversation.

In *How to Live in Fear*, Lance Hahn shares his story of discovering the impact of anxiety disorders upon his life, his family, and ministry. Make no mistake: his analysis is raw and forthright. The pain and devastation associated with this illness is very real, even for those of us in ministry. Yet this conversation gives us hope as he helps us navigate the emotional, spiritual, and relational turmoil present in the lives of people of all ethnicities, socio-economic status, cultures, and faiths.

My conversation with the young lady at the thrift store affirmed two things to me. First, top finds can indeed be found in the most dark and obscure places. Second, transparency and honesty reveal what is often hidden away in casual conversation. Our fears should not serve as walls of shame; rather, they are bridges that connect all of our stories.

How to Live in Fear connects our stories. It's a top find!

—Parnell M. Lovelace Jr., MSW, DMin

PANIC, PROVIDENCE, AND THE PASTOR

I thought I was going insane.

My brain felt as though it were splitting in half.

I struggled just to breathe.

My mind raced, and my thoughts were jumbled and murky.

I couldn't talk with anyone; dealing with people was virtually impossible.

I felt I couldn't worship or even pray.

The peace of God seemed a million miles away, totally out of my reach.

Life was excruciating and my fears so incredibly debilitating.

A person can take only so much.

I'm a Christian. I love Jesus. In fact, I'm a pastor of a large church where—week in and week out—I teach thousands of people the truths of God. I believe in His grace, healing, and powers of deliverance. I believe He loves me and wants the absolute best for my life.

But on an all-too-frequent basis, I suffer greatly from panic disorder. Overwhelming fear grips my soul and won't let up—for hours, sometimes days, even weeks. I totally get David's dark language often used throughout Psalms, in passages such as this one:

> My heart is in anguish within me;
>> the terrors of death have fallen on me.
> Fear and trembling have beset me;
>> horror has overwhelmed me.
> I said, "Oh, that I had the wings of a dove!
>> I would fly away and be at rest.
> I would flee far away
>> and stay in the desert;
> I would hurry to my place of shelter,
>> far from the tempest and storm. (Ps. 55:4–8 NIV)

While the psalmist likely wasn't describing a panic attack, the bottom line is that he was suffering—suffering at a level he wanted to run from but couldn't escape because the enemy he was battling the most was inside his own soul.

In the pages of this book, I want to share my story with you—a tale of salvation, redemption, and favor, coupled with the reality of my ongoing battle with an often-debilitating medical condition that began at age six.

A prevailing belief in our Western church culture is that God will keep bad things from happening to good people, especially His people. But according to Scripture—regardless of which theological circles we belong to—this man-made paradigm is not true. It never was and never will be. We've seen, heard, and experienced too many bad things happening to good people—even to Christians, even to us—too many times.

In fact, much of life feels like a battle. Maybe that's why my struggle with panic and fear has, for so many years, produced a huge measure of doubt, questioning, and even feelings of abandonment.

Perhaps you have been diagnosed with panic disorder, experience panic attacks, or at the very least feel as though you wrestle with fear more than the average person does. Maybe the phrase "freaking out" in the book's subtitle caught your eye, and you feel those words describe how you live more often than you want to admit. Or maybe you picked up this book because your spouse, child, parent, relative, or friend suffers from this condition and you want to better understand how to sympathize with, minister to, and love on that person. May God bless you for caring on such a deep level. I hope you find clarity and encouragement here to help your loved one.

Regardless, I pray you find comfort, community, and counsel in these pages.

Now that straight out of the gate you have a good understanding of my faith in God, my pastoral credentials, and my level of panic and fear, I want to make one thing crystal clear to those of you who are suffering in fear: *I know how you feel.*

This statement of empathy is so important to me to get across to you.

I know how you feel.

You might not believe anyone could possibly understand, but I do.

As a matter of fact—and to be completely transparent— the main reason I wrote this book was to say those five words to those who suffer from fear. Why else would I want to confess the worst part of my life and some of my most embarrassing moments when, as a pastor of a large congregation and member of an awesome family, I could have written about my blessings—all the feel-good stuff many pastors have written about successfully?

In the land of anxiety and panic, not many people are willing to talk openly and candidly—especially in the church—so I will. Sure, we'd all rather hide behind an "I'm fine" in the church hallway than confess the truth: "I'm hurting." But I want to change that. For you. Here and now.

For those of us who have panic attacks, on our best days we're physically miserable; on our worst days, we feel like sub-par Christians. If the Bible says we need not be anxious, then why are we? If Jesus is our solid Rock and Fortress, then why do we feel as if we're living on sand in isolation? If Jesus can calm the wind and waves, why can't He calm the tempest in our hearts? And for goodness' sake, why doesn't He take the fear away? Just deliver us, heal us?

Decade after decade I've asked these questions. You probably have too. I've tried everything, followed almost every recommendation, and yet here I am, still a broken man—successful and strong by the world's standards but often feeling like a scared child within. I influence the lives of thousands upon thousands but can't eliminate panic attacks in my own life. Recognized and respected preachers have told me I'm not "accessing the kingdom," or I "don't have enough faith," or I haven't "really read the Word," but by the very token that they would say such things, I know they've never faced what I have. The fact remains: I *know* I am a child of God—and I'm *still* scared.

My hope is that five things will happen in your own heart as you read:

1. You will be overwhelmed by the presence of God and come to believe He is with you on your journey.
2. You will be deeply encouraged that there are millions of your brothers and sisters walking alongside you, with you, supporting you.
3. You will experience a freedom to realize your fear does not have to *define* you nor *confine* you.
4. You will not merely *survive* life with anxiety but learn to *thrive* in and through the storms.
5. You will learn how to truly live, even in fear, because there is so much life God has for you to embrace, even in the midst of your struggle.

My personal goals for this book are to

1. Provide help for the hurting, while making no guarantees.

Since he himself has gone through suffering and testing, he is able to help us when we are being tested. (Heb. 2:18 NLT)

I wish I could say that if you read this book you will no longer suffer from anxiety. I can't make that promise. But, as evidenced in my own life, I do think you will find divine help *in* your suffering, not a personal cure *from* your suffering. I've read plenty of books that make promises for healing, only to find that not only does the author *not* suffer from fear, anxiety, or panic attacks but he or she doesn't even *understand* the condition. I do suffer; I do understand; I want to encourage you by sharing my story, along with everything that has helped me.

2. Shut down the bullies.

> Live, GOD! Blessings from my Rock,
>> my free and freeing God, towering!
> This God set things right for me
>> and shut up the people who talked back.
> He rescued me from enemy anger,
>> he pulled me from the grip of upstarts,
> He saved me from the bullies. (Ps. 18:46–48 THE MESSAGE)

Growing up in the church culture, I have had far too much interaction with sharp-tongued, religious bruisers who declare if you struggle then somehow you are a weak Christian. If this is true, what do you do with the words of David and others in Scripture who vocally battled invisible enemies on an emotional, mental, and spiritual level? And why would God decide to place those cries and confessions right smack in the middle of His Book?

3. Bring hope to your heart.

> You, too, must be patient. Take courage, for the coming of the Lord is near. (James 5:8 NLT)

Take courage, my friend. You are not alone. God has not abandoned you. He is walking with you. Your suffering doesn't mean you aren't saved. You are gloriously adopted as God's child. You are not the only one who doubts and hurts. We are all on different journeys, but together, no matter how dark and long the tunnel might get, we can behold the beautiful bright Light at the end and run to Him.

In fact, I invite you now to run with me. Let's do this! Let me share with you what I've learned about how to live in fear and mastering the art of freaking out.

PART 1

LIVING IN FEAR:
MY STORY

I want to share my story with you through the filter of my fear. My desire before I offer help, counsel, and ministry is to open up and allow you to hear my pain, my struggles, and what this battle with fear has created in my own life.

CHAPTER 1

WHY ME, LORD?

My anxiety keeps me from enjoying things
as much as I should at this age.
—Amanda Seyfried, actress[1]

At just six years old, all I could feel was sheer terror. My throat constricted. I couldn't breathe. I was gagging as though some unseen force were strangling me. *Why is this happening?* raced through my young mind. Little kids might get ear infections and stomachaches, but nothing like this should happen. Why me? And why couldn't anyone help?

Just make it stop!

This scene occurred too many times on too many days. I wasn't actually choking on anything; my throat would just lock up. In the 1970s, the medical and psychological world didn't yet understand panic attacks or anxiety issues. And my parents didn't know what to do.

I grew up in a charismatic Christian home, and my family

did the only thing they could think of: they took me to the elders of the church for prayer.

I had spent every Sunday I could remember at that church—an old theater that had been converted into a house of worship. I never wanted to go to Sunday school, so instead I sat with my parents and older siblings in the main service. Like most kids, I would entertain myself. I drew little cartoon animals and passed them over to my brother, who was eight years older than me, and he would name each one. Sometimes my sister and I played a connect-the-dots game on paper, trying to see who could score the most points by the time church ended. Occasionally, we would sit in the small balcony section, which I thought was cool. Right after the worship band finished their songs, the pastor would preach from the raised theater stage.

I remember that particular prayer-for-healing experience. I followed my parents to an upper room over the fellowship hall, where a group of middle-aged men—most of whom I didn't know—was waiting for me. What were they going to do? What was about to happen?

They were nice enough; they even smiled some. But I was nervous. There were no cartoon animals or dot games in this meeting—just the elders praying. They pleaded with Jesus to take away whatever was ailing me. Each of them laid hands on me and prayed simple, yet heartfelt prayers. They made brief mentions of demons, as I recall. Not a very pleasant experience for a six-year-old kid, yet far less dramatic than my mind had conceived. There was a lot of love and concern. I made it through, and I was glad when it was over and we could leave.

I wish I could tell you the Lord swept in and rescued that

little guy from his torment, but that was not to be. Over time, the choking did subside. Unfortunately, the symptoms began to change their manifestation, moving from my throat to my stomach.

The human body has an amazing ability to store stress and fear in the pit of its midsection—what often in slang is called our "gut." Nausea ruined many a meal and many a day for me, often hitting when I was ready to go to school. Feeling as though I were going to vomit made me miss a lot of sleepovers and hijacked my spot at a lot of parties. Even when I did feel better, I worried that the nausea would return, leaving me in a vulnerable state. Although I never fully understood this nagging condition, I did find that if I stayed home the feelings would slowly dissipate.

By the time I was ten years old, I realized something emotional was at play. Whatever was going on wasn't merely a physical ailment.

—

I begged my mom to not make me go. I pleaded. I cried. I knew full well that a ten-year-old boy shouldn't be acting like this, but I was terrified! What does a kid that age do when he is scared to death? Reason goes out the window.

I pressed myself against the orange interior door of our brown Pinto station wagon as I sobbed.

Where was I being forced to go, you ask? Was it to juvenile detention? Maybe to the doctor for shots? To the tailor's to be fit for a suit?

No. It was the grocery store.

What could possibly create terror in the heart of a boy in such a place?

I was scared of getting beat up, apparently by roving bands of grocery gangs. I was scared I would die in there.

But what was all this drama about? These were such odd issues coming from a boy who grew up in a peaceful home in a sleepy small town with not a single moment of abuse or violence.

This wasn't an isolated incident. During this season of my life, my mom had this battle of wills on her hands every time she tried to stop somewhere on the way home from school. She didn't understand, and I couldn't help her at all because I felt completely out of control.

I remember the day my mom went from coaxing to bribery in an attempt to get me to go to the mall to buy new jeans at Miller's Outpost. I was a growing boy, and all my pants were riding up my legs. I also had holes in the knees, which might be stylish today but definitely wasn't back then. Yet my fear of public spaces and crowds was so severe that I would have rather faced the jeers of my peers because of outgrown clothes than face the horrors of the mall crowd. At first my mom tried promising that it would be the fastest shopping experience known to man; then she tried to hype up the after-party at the ice cream store. But I wasn't having any of it. No manner of her begging could get my eyes off the monster of fear in front of me.

The definition of *phobia* is "a persistent, abnormal, and irrational fear of a specific thing or situation that compels one to avoid it, despite the awareness and reassurance that it is not dangerous."[2] Nailed it! That's exactly how I felt.

And just when I thought life couldn't possibly get worse, it did.

—

Around the age of fourteen, there was a week or so when I couldn't even leave the house—at all.

I couldn't go to school.

I couldn't step outside with my friends.

I was emotionally bound by the four walls of my home.

But just as the fear entered unannounced, the feelings subsided without much fanfare. Thankfully, after that week or so, the invisible gates somehow opened, and I felt free to move around within my limited, secure spaces: school, home, neighborhood, friends' houses, and maybe one store—places I had previously deemed safe.

As I grew older, however, even in those safe settings my anxiety would unpredictably find a way to break in (or out, depending on your perspective). Some of my biggest fears began to invade my most secure spot—my own home. I grew up in the 1980s, during the Cold War era, also known as the Nuclear Age. The standoff between Superpower America and Mother Russia was propagated like a Wild West duel—two gunfighters staring each other down to see who would draw his weapon first. And of course, someone was going to die—if not both of them.

Everywhere I turned, on TV and radio programs, in magazines and newspapers, the foreboding possibilities of World War III were emblazoned before the masses—and specifically before me. I learned that an atomic explosion would begin with an incinerating blast that I couldn't possibly outrun, no matter what fast car I might be driving. Once the explosion struck, I would see the mushroom cloud. With nowhere to hide, I would have a few scant moments to reflect on my life before being obliterated into dust.

I, Lance, would then be a smoldering dust bunny. That's all I needed to think about to live in fear, and too often it was all I *did* think about.

During the same decade, the evangelical church at large regularly used fear as a marketing device. Maybe it was to capitalize on the Cold War fears. After all, people were thinking about the end of the world and about dying, so why not connect that to faith?

Those in my own Christian circle—our church, my parents—believed the end of the world was imminent and could happen at any moment. And so did I. If the nuclear warheads didn't get you, you were destined to be *left behind* if you weren't right with God. Every religious tract talked about the Antichrist, the mark of the Beast, families separated in the Rapture, and the terrible ravages of God's wrath.

Yippee! I was a little, sensitive guy battling fear on a daily basis; trying to grow up in an already scary world was entirely too much for me to handle. More mornings than I can count, I would wake up to a naturally red sky outside my bedroom window, and panic would overtake me. To me, that blood-colored dawn meant either the bombs had been dropped or Jesus had just returned. The fact that I was still there in my warm bed meant that I had been abandoned, and my terrorized little brain scrambled to figure out a way a boy my age could survive, especially if even God was now against me.

—

It was 1986, and I was so honored that my brother had asked fifteen-year-old me to be a groomsman at his wedding. Dressed in a tuxedo, I was standing with his buddies onstage in the chapel on the campus of the University of the Pacific in Stockton, California—in the middle of summer with no air-conditioning. My parents were sitting in the front row with my sister. It was so cool to stand with my brother on one of the most important days of his life. The chapel was filled with guests waiting to hear "I do" and see my brother kiss his bride. I was as excited as anyone, but also nervous.

Just as the happy couple turned to face each other to begin the ceremony, I began to feel woozy. I knew the danger of locking my knees, so I bent them slightly, shifting my weight back and forth from one foot to the other. But my vision started to go, and the signs of fainting must have appeared on my face because one of the groomsmen leaned in and asked, "Are you okay, Lance?"

People's heads had appeared to grow sizably over the last few minutes, like distorted Dr. Seuss characters, and I could barely stand.

I answered, "No, I don't think so." Then my vision went dark, like a fading light—and I went down.

The next thing I knew I was seeing a bright light. Not heaven, but the doors to the outside of the chapel. My father was carrying me, and he kept saying over and over, "Hang in there, son." Apparently, when I collapsed on stage I started to convulse. Within moments of being laid down on the grass under a tree, I heard sirens. Two shimmering red emergency vehicles drove up with their air horns drowning out my brother's vows to his new bride. The wedding went on without me, and I was no longer standing beside my brother where I so wanted to be.

Nothing like making a moment more memorable, right?

—

In the middle of my teen years, when so many suffer some of the worst angst of their lives, I finally found some relief. My first significant period of freedom from anxiety began when I was sixteen. In fact, the peace lasted almost uninterrupted for about six years. Why? I got my driver's license. Freedom and control were mine in a way I had never experienced before.

Suddenly I was the one who determined when and where I went. I was calling the shots, and if I didn't want to stop somewhere I didn't have to. I was free to escape from any situation I deemed anxious and fearful. When the steering wheel was put into my own hands, I didn't have to face as many of those fears. I had an escape route in nearly every situation—at least for a season, before the overwhelming fear eventually pushed its way back into my life.

In my early twenties, my anxiety returned. For instance, I was able to go shopping at the mall, but I needed to take breaks to go outside, clear my head, and regain perspective. As I went from store to store, my vision would start to get blurry. I felt almost dizzy, though not quite disoriented. I never imagined I would be retreating from crowds instead of being energized by them, because I'm a people person. I love people! I already loved public speaking. But somehow my body didn't agree with my mind, or maybe my mind didn't agree with my heart. The stomachaches that had bothered me so much as a boy came back with a vengeance as my body continued to hold fear in the core of my being.

One of the most maddening things about struggling with fear is the constant question "Why?" I was plagued with thoughts of what I might have done wrong. Shame followed me around like a looming shadow. I didn't know one other soul who felt the way I felt. I felt alone. I felt like a freak.

Why was I picked to win the lottery of doom?

Why was I afraid of what I was afraid of?

Why me? Why me, God?

CHAPTER 2

THE AGITATING ANGST
OF ADULTHOOD

I try not to worry about the future . . . so I take
each day just one anxiety attack at a time!!
—Tom Wilson, cartoonist[1]

In 1996, my wife, Suzi, and I were newlyweds. We decided to
scrape together all the money we could and book a cruise with
our good friends, the Patelzicks. We could only afford the
minimal three-day voyage from Orange County to Catalina
Island, down to Ensenada, Mexico, and back.

I had never been on a cruise before and was looking forward
to a getaway from the world. I daydreamed about how relaxing
those seventy-two hours would be, out on the ocean, soaking up
the sun, and exploring the two port cities. Greg and Mindy were
fired up to go exploring, so the four of us set off on our adventure.

The first day we had an awesome time, laughing and

swapping stories, eating lots of food, and taking advantage of all the fun on the ship. The next morning we arrived off the coast of Catalina. I could not wait to see this beautiful island I had heard so much about from so many people. I hoped the romance of the environment would overwhelm my new bride. And I was pumped to get to visit the former spring training facility the Chicago Cubs had used to prepare for their baseball seasons for thirty years, view the former home of Norma Jeane Mortenson (aka Marilyn Monroe), and walk where stars, celebrities, and sports heroes had walked.

When I woke up on the day of the Catalina excursion, something wasn't right. I felt off and didn't quite know what was going on. Not overly concerned, I figured it would go away. I wasn't on any medication and didn't know enough yet about anxiety to pick up on the signals, so I forged ahead like a good soldier. I didn't want to let down the team; after all, this was an amazing vacation and we had spent all our extra money to get there.

Because the shoreline is too shallow for the ship to dock safely, our excursion would start with taking a smaller boat to shore. On the short ride to the island, the sensations went from uncomfortable to immobilizing. I had never had such a rapid onset with this set of symptoms, but I felt dizzy, scared, and sick to my stomach. By the time we reached land, the attack was so severe that I told my wife and our friends to go on without me. It took some convincing, but they agreed. I quickly got on the next boat back to the ship and beelined straight for our cabin. At first, I paced around the tiny closet-sized room, and then I tried lying down.

What is happening to me? I kept thinking. With my heart

racing, my thoughts flying at warp speed, I was convinced I was having a heart attack. I didn't know if a twenty-four-year-old healthy man could have a heart attack, but I didn't want to take the risk.

I called the ship's doctor. The woman who answered said they had just encountered an emergency and were swamped. Could I call back?

But I didn't. The rational side of my mind kicked in and told me how ridiculous I was being and that I wasn't going to have a heart attack, no matter what I felt.

Slowly, gradually, relief seeped in. I even tried to nap. By the time Suzi and our friends came back, I was mostly better, but the trip was now spoiled for me. My disorder decided to set itself off that day for no discernible reason, so I was wary the next two days as well.

One of the great hassles of living with fear is how much it takes us away from being fully present with our families, especially after we have children. It feels so selfish to want to be anywhere else but smack in the middle of a loved one's birthday party or piano recital or wedding. Just as depression might take a parent away from the family room and leave that mom or dad alone in a darkened bedroom, so too does anxiety remove us from being emotionally present.

———

I had hardly slept at all. Getting up, I felt like death warmed over, and my eyes stung. In just a few hours, more than a thousand people would be gathering in our main sanctuary to hear me preach, and my sanity was hanging by a wire.

I didn't know if I was going to make it. Seriously.

No one is good at dealing with loss, especially death— least of all me.

I went through the motions of ironing my clothes and set out for the church.

I knew I couldn't talk to anyone about what happened the night before without falling apart, so I kept it to myself at first. Worship was finishing up onstage as I sat in my office waiting to head into the sanctuary. My chest started to tighten.

I hadn't been able to get a deep breath all morning, but now it was getting worse. Fatigue washed over me in waves, and the fight-or-flight symptoms of my panic disorder began to overtake me.

In a daze, I forced myself to go into the sanctuary, and as I prepared to walk onto the stage, I felt my legs go numb. I was going to collapse. I told my assistant to get the band ready to do another worship set if I couldn't continue. I also asked her to get another pastor on standby to jump in, in case I couldn't finish. As she dashed off, the announcement videos were winding down. I forced myself up the stairs and clutched the lectern. As the lights came up and one thousand pairs of eyes locked on me, I was fully exposed with no place to run.

What should I do?

I decided to come clean. I told the congregation what was happening. *I was having a full-blown panic attack from my body being too wiped out and from the emotional impact of the night before.*

Here's how I got there:

My dog's name was Sammi—short for Samantha. Even though she never knew any better, she was definitely a mutt.

When my wife and I first brought Sammi home, she was pure white and had eyes set wide like a pit bull puppy. Our not-so-expert guess was that she was about six months old, but we never knew for sure because we adopted her from the local animal shelter. The goal was for her to be a buddy to our female beagle named Frankie (we apparently have a thing for naming girl dogs with boy names).

Well, the plan didn't work. The two canines didn't end up getting along. We found an extraordinary home for Frankie and kept little Sammi so we could focus on raising the once-abandoned dog.

It didn't take long to see that Sammi had a natural instinct for herding. No sheep or cattle were around, so she herded the only wayward ones she had available—our children. When the kids went down the stairs, she would lean in to steer them. Sammi was consistently at my feet and followed me everywhere. We found out later that she was part Australian Shepherd cattle dog (although she had no obvious accent in her bark).

To me, Sammi was the coolest dog ever. She wasn't the most attractive with her yellow and beige blotches, but she was *my* dog. In fact, as the years passed, she all but wrote off the rest of the family and made me the center of her life. Her life's mission was to watch over and protect me 24/7. Wherever I was, in or outside our home, she was right there. Sammi was a constant source of joy and laughter, even with her untimely "gas releases" at dinner parties. Always the quintessential embodiment of "man's best friend," she became one of my best and most loyal friends—for fifteen and a half years.

Other than my wife, there was no one else I spent more time with and who relied on me so heavily for comfort and well-being. And as crazy as it seemed, the older Sammi got and the more she went downhill, the more she made her way into my heart. Every act of love came with difficulty, yet she never faltered. I highly value sacrificial dedication, and my dog was the epitome of that to me.

Let me stop here to say that if you have a dog or some other pet in your family, I know you get this story. No explanation needed. A wise person once said, "Until one has loved an animal, a part of one's soul remains unawakened." If you have a pet close to your heart, you know that full well. If you aren't a pet person, this story might be a bit difficult to understand. But I ask you to press on with me here, because the point is that grief and sadness, from whatever source, can be violent triggers for panic and anxiety.

After a long afternoon and evening of preaching at our Saturday services, I came home exhausted. I put my feet up to watch some mindless reality show about cooking and eat a bowl of ice cream. At 10:45 p.m., Sammi tried to come down the stairs to join me. Suddenly I heard a sickening *thump, thump, thump* as my dog tripped midway down the stairs and tumbled to the wooden floor below. My stomach turned as I heard her startled yelp, and I dashed around the corner to her. There she lay up against the wall with her legs spread out straight, not moving. Her eyes were wide open, and I could tell she was scared. I thought she was paralyzed. I prayed that God would help her not feel pain. I wanted to make her comfortable so I could make some decisions about what to do.

Despite the late hour, I phoned my mom to come watch the kids, who were asleep upstairs, and my wife and I rushed Sammi to the only vet who was willing to see us in our late-night emergency. My worst fears were confirmed as the vet delivered the bad news: "I'm sorry, but there is nothing we can do. You need to say good-bye to Sammi tonight."

I stroked my faithful companion's fur while the injection did its work, and Sammi drifted peacefully to sleep for the last time. When I walked out that door into the night, I fell apart. I cried more than I ever remember crying in my life. Like I said, I know this might sound silly to those of you who don't love animals the way I do. I know she was "just" a dog, but she was *my* dog, my friend, the best.

When we got home that night, I wept for more than an hour. As the tears fell, I walked and talked it out with God. In the midst of my pain, He was so kind to me. One half of my mind wanted to fall apart from the loss of my best friend, and the other had this bizarre, deep-seated peace about how Sammi's end had come. God had made sure I was there when she fell. I was able to comfort her as she faced the pain and confusion of her final hours. I was the one to make the tough decision. I was there as she slipped off into the most peaceful sleep of her life. And even in that moment, God was protecting my fragile heart, proving once again that He is good—even in terrible times.

Now back to that Sunday morning at church.

It didn't matter to me that I was on the verge of collapse. I didn't have time to get someone else to speak, and I always try my hardest not to walk away from a fight. I determined to go as far as I could, and if I gave in to the effects of my disorder and passed out, that would be in God's hands. The congregation could see something was wrong, and I had prepared them for such a moment as this by sharing my battle with anxiety publicly and often. I knew they could handle it and support me.

Sure enough, as I shared what had happened, how I was feeling, and that I was operating in panic, I saw their faces soften. Some people even began to tear up. I had hardly finished recounting my manifestations of fear when a woman in the front row stood up and said loud enough for all to hear, "Can we pray for you right now, Pastor?" Her voice was saturated in love and concern.

What could I do? I didn't want the moment to be all about me and to take the focus off the Lord and His Word. I didn't want to allow my weakness to be the center of attention. But then again, why not? Was this what He wanted, to use my struggle in people's lives? Why not humble myself and allow my congregation to minister to me? Why not let the Lord's grace flow through their love and into my heart? Why not let them care for me the way they desired to do? If I was only a man, as I had often said from the platform, then perhaps it was only right to let them support me.

They prayed for me.

I prayed with them.

After that moment of vulnerability and the enveloping love I felt, I thanked them, turned to my notes, and began to preach in faith, with no guarantees of getting better.

In supernatural fashion, as He has so often done, God wrapped His arms around me and carried me through the rest of the service. With each passing minute, my chest loosened a little more, my body began to relax, and my voice became stronger, clearer. I could feel the dark fog of panic dissolving from my mind. But I still had one last service to preach, an

"Ask Pastor Lance" live Q&A session for an hour, and then a lunch with an important job candidate for our staff.

I'm sure that was an unexpected treat for him to experience that morning. "Surprise! The senior pastor here has massive anxiety disorder, and this is not the first time this has happened. How's your sushi? Would you like to come on board?"

Nevertheless, for the rest of that marathon day, God sustained me. The prayers of the people I pastor, lifted up in love and concern for me, were answered again.

Through my brokenness God has crafted a congregation in which I am free to share my troubles from the stage and others are free to share their troubles with me and one another. The church has provided a safe place—albeit a large one—for me to be as I learn how to live in fear. We must not let our shame keep us quiet. People around us who also love us want to know what's happening in our hearts. It's vital that we express our fear to those around us so they can help us. Whether it's nervousness or a panic attack, when anxiety strikes, it's natural to want to isolate, to run away and put our heads in the proverbial sand. Unfortunately, when we isolate and retreat inward, we are left to our own thoughts, which have seemingly taken on a life of their own. When we feel trapped and alone, the fear gives way to more fear, and the giant snowball of panic crushes logic and reason as it continues to grow. A safe place, however, breaks the cycle and lets off some of the steam driving the anxiety engine.

When I told the congregation, two important things occurred. First, they sought help from almighty God by interceding for me. Nothing and no one is more able to dismantle an anxiety bomb like God's truth and power. Second, by exposing my fear out loud to them, I pulled back the curtain so everyone knew what was happening in my life. I no longer had to hide my pain. I didn't have to shove it deeper down, where it would only fester and grow. I didn't have to lie to cover up why I was behaving the way I was. It also put them on notice so that whatever happened next made sense. They had a context for my behavior and could see that even pastors have problems.

In retrospect, I hoped that my visible torment would allow at least a few secret sufferers to feel less alone. And it did. I received countless letters, notes, and e-mails from church members telling me how they could relate to what I went through and how knowing about it helped them feel less alone. And in the process I was set free from the cage of my own fear.

As I faced my fears head-on and brought them into the light, I was able to see them more clearly and get past them. Perhaps you haven't felt confident enough to share your pain with others. I beg you to reconsider. Fear diminishes in the light, and anxiety loosens its grip when we have help. That morning after I confessed in church, I was able to see past myself and begin to care for those in front of me. Out of my pain, God brought peace and even joy. As the pressure of fear receded, I became myself again. I was able to get into my groove of preaching, and the burden in my heart began to lift. My spiritual gift of sarcasm returned. I began to tell my funny stories again and be more lighthearted. The more I smiled real smiles, the more I felt sweet freedom return to my life.

CHAPTER 3

MY DARKEST HOUR

*The worst evils of life are those which do not
exist except in our imagination. If we had
no troubles but real troubles, we should not
have a tenth part of our present sorrows.*
—Charles Spurgeon, theologian[1]

Nothing had prepared me for what was to come at the beginning of 2014—for the sheer duration and the intensity of the tsunami that was quietly barreling at breakneck speed to overwhelm my world. Maybe I should have seen it coming, if I'd only noticed the handwriting on the wall. But how do you anticipate the perfect storm? Even right now, in this moment, I can't go back to that dark place without completely unnerving my present.

I have survived many panic attacks—even a few that lasted for a day or so. But forty days? Day after day of not being able to get a deep breath; not being able to think clearly;

not being able to go to work; not being able to interact with people around me without intense effort; not being able to worship or pray or have any semblance of peace. Even in small moments of relief, my level of fear never got below a 4 on a scale of 1 to 10.

I was already due for a sabbatical. I was tired and weary. The church was in turmoil because God was shaking things up, and I was the guy sitting in the driver's seat. After fifteen and a half years of leading the church with a solid, biblical approach, I found that trust in my leadership had begun to unravel in six short months because of changes I made in spiritual and ministerial methodology that I felt were necessary. My reputation was challenged. My friends and coleaders were vilified. My connections with other churches were held suspect. All hell was breaking loose, so to speak. People were leaving the church without knowing the facts. Friends who held leadership positions in our church turned their backs and walked out without even talking to me. To say it was a mess was an understatement.

I'm not blaming God, although I think He started it. Honestly, my team and I could have done many things better to lead through this period. We own that. I own that. We could have handled this season better had we been more solid as a leadership team, but that's where things only got worse.

One of our most important staff members, someone who was key to our decision-making process and ran the majority of the senior leadership areas, stepped down from ministry. Bookkeeping slid into a temporary chaos and a spending freeze was put into effect. All the while, we were in the early stages of our planned long-term capital campaign for the new

$14 million campus we were going to purchase. Our elder team was stressed and agitated. We were at each other's throats.

You would think I could have found something else to do for a living, but honestly, even as bad as I felt, I couldn't fathom doing anything other than being a pastor. Usually I'm the confident guy who thinks he can lead any group out of anything, but in those days I was struggling to just hold myself together.

All my major emotional and anxiety triggers were firing—betrayal, misunderstanding, loneliness, isolation, spiritual attack, fears of a slipping sanity, and physical health issues. The works. I could not even imagine ever feeling normal again.

After a week or so of staying home on sick leave, I realized the situation wasn't going to subside anytime soon. The first thing I had to do was get some of the other pastors on staff to cover for me in the pulpit, and then I would cancel all my meetings and speaking engagements. To honor my commitment to transparency, I pushed through my humiliation and drafted a letter to convey to my staff that, at the critical moment they needed their leader the most, he was in the fetal position at home, freaking out.

I was embarrassed; no, actually, I was horrified. I felt so guilty about placing all the weight of responsibility on their shoulders. The executive pastor, my personal assistant and coleader, various ministry team leaders, a few staff members, key volunteers, and I were all leaving our posts at the same time. Most of those exits were either necessary or involuntary, so I'm not blaming anyone; it was just one of those seasons. Perhaps what frustrated me most was that usually I'm the "iron man," who works no matter how sick he gets and will preach with a fever, if need be. I'm usually the strong one, but in those days I couldn't gather my wits to even leave the house.

Weeks passed, and my situation continued to be horrendous. I remember one evening when my two daughters, my wife, and I were sprawled out on our California-king-size bed in the master bedroom. We were watching the movie *Miracle*, the story about the 1980 US Olympic Men's Hockey Team. I thought watching the film would help me. Usually family movie night is a highlight for me, because I love movies so much and I get to cuddle up with my family. But this evening there was no warm and fuzzy in sight.

For the life of me, I hadn't been able to take a deep breath for days. Even though I was just lying there on my side of the bed and trying to pay attention to the movie, I could not fill my lungs no matter what position I took.

I felt as though a thousand-pound boulder were on my chest. The sense of suffocation is unnerving to say the least; it's a big panic trigger for me. I did my best to remain calm. I used every breathing technique I had been taught. I knew most instances of passing out during panic attacks have to do with an inability to control breathing. But this time it didn't matter. I was getting light-headed.

I didn't want to worry my girls, so I made up some excuse for needing to leave the room and practically ran outside once I was out of their sight. I paced back and forth in our small backyard, trying to get a grip. I prayed and prayed. I texted friends to ask for prayer. I worshiped. I begged. I tried to take thoughts captive, knowing my problem was all in my mind. I tried to distract myself, to think about anything other than not being able to breathe. But the panic wouldn't lift. No strategy I had learned was even making a dent.

I paced outside for about thirty minutes until I realized that although I still couldn't breathe very well, I wasn't going to pass out. Being miserable by myself outside was no better than being miserable in my bed with my family. I went back upstairs and did my best to listen to what Coach Kurt Russell had to say.

It was nights like this when Suzi would shift into protector mode and ask me if I wanted to pray. If I am honest, I have to say I didn't want to pray anymore. I didn't even know if I could handle listening to prayer without freaking out. Maybe you've experienced this—your nerves are so high-strung that anything serious, important, or that demands you to be emotionally present is too much to handle. That's how I am about praying when I'm in the middle of a panic attack and someone wants to pray with me. I can't focus on praying; I'm spending all my energy trying to stop myself from running around screaming like a little girl.

At the same time, another conversation in my head reminded me that the most difficult battles are fought with prayer and worship. God was my hope, not my problem. His power is made greater in my suffering. I knew that. He didn't need me to strain in prayer, only receive. I agreed to let Suzi pray over me, and I lay down on our bed. The little ones had gone to sleep, and my wife went to get her Bible. For the next forty-five minutes, she sat next to me, rubbed my chest with one hand, and held the Bible in the other, reading chapter after chapter of truth while I focused on breathing and remaining sane.

Eventually enough peace came through that she could stop, and I was able to drift off to sleep. We had many of those nights. Never before had Suzi emerged as such a powerhouse of prayer and spiritual leadership as she did in that season, and it's one of the beautiful blessings God redeemed out of a difficult time.

As the weeks of anxiety wore on, no one knew what to do. Suzi had walked this road with me many times in the past, but almost all of them were contained and handled without too much effect on the household. This time was entirely different. By now the kids knew something was wrong with Dad. My parents, in-laws, and siblings were aware and praying for me. Most of them were scared, too, because they had never seen me like this before. No matter how much they tried to hide their true feelings, I could tell they were afraid, and that only added to my fears.

I did everything I could to fight. All I knew to do was to try to pull through.

I asked members of the congregation, my staff, my friends, and my personal intercession team to intercede for me. Pastors from other churches offered to come to my house and pray over me. I called upon every source of help I could. I even raised my medication to the highest level I was comfortable taking and saw my doctor multiple times. But the panic wouldn't stop. Instead of abating, the disorder seemed to be growing. How much worse could it get?

And then came the day when life went from terrible to catastrophic. My fear was at an all-time high. I was pacing around the house and mumbling to myself. The level was a 10 out of 10. I couldn't take it anymore. I went upstairs to get away from everyone, put on some worship music, and began to cry out to God for help. This time, however, with every stanza of worship music, my condition worsened. I could feel my sanity slipping away. I desperately wanted to escape. I couldn't flee from myself, but there was no one else to fight. No matter where I went, there I was.

I was being utterly consumed by fear, tension, stress, and panic. I quickly found that I couldn't even form the words to pray anymore. No relief. Somehow my mind was so distorted that every thought of God brought a sense of doom and fear. I could only picture judgment, rejection, and anger from my Lord. God, my only hope and help, became the manifested form of my fear. If there was ever evidence of spiritual attack intensifying my anxiety, this moment was the pinnacle.

I eventually shut off the worship music. I lay there and shook and cried, but even crying couldn't adequately express the intensity of my emotions.

It was the darkest hour of my life.

I pray that the Lord heals me or takes me home before I ever face anything like that again.

PART 2

LIVING IN FEAR: OUR JOURNEY TOGETHER

Now that you have read my story from childhood to adulthood—through the lens of my panic disorder, fear, and anxiety—here is some practical information I have learned along the way that has helped me. I want to break it down and help you apply as much as possible to your own life as we journey together through our fear.

If we are afflicted with such trouble and pain, *then know it is so that you might ultimately experience comfort and salvation. If we experience comfort, it is to encourage you so that you can hold up while you endure the same sufferings we all share. Remember that our hope for you stands firm,* unshaken and unshakable. *That's because we know that as you share in our sufferings, so you will also share in our comfort. (2 Cor. 1:6–7 THE VOICE)*

CHAPTER 4

THE FEAR WE SHARE

There are people who have the glass half full
and glass half empty, and I'm afraid the glass is
going to break and I'll cut myself on the shards.
—Scott Stossel, journalist and editor[1]

The triggers for your fear are likely very different from mine, but the end result probably feels much the same to us both. The sources might be different, but the fear itself we share.

There is a vast difference between sympathy and empathy. If a friend of yours loses a family member to a tragic accident, but you have never experienced such a loss, the best you can do is *sympathize*. Why? Because you don't know that particular pain firsthand, yet you can offer a hug and your heart to help. But if you, too, have suffered this type of loss, you can *empathize*. You have experienced this pain and know the road of grief well.

If you are a relative or friend of someone who suffers from

fear, you are reading this book to better understand and sympathize in a deeper manner. But if you are a fellow sufferer, you and I are offering empathy to each other. We get it. We *feel* the pain. We *know* the pain. Therefore, we *share* the pain.

I'm going to continue to drive this point home: my deepest care and prayer is that you find hope and help in these pages.

Hope—that great sense and longing that life will get better.

Help—tools to actually make life better.

These two forces working in synergy can bring true change to our lives.

THREE KEYS TO UNDERSTANDING

What in the world causes panic, fear, and anxiety? There is power in knowing all you can about your situation. While you might never be an expert on fear, you can become an expert on *your* fear. Seeking and figuring out answers for yourself can bring a greater understanding, if not actual healing.

The reason for our fear is indeed crucial information for us to own. I want to share from a thirty-thousand-foot perspective what I believe is going on. Whether you are a chronic worrier, have a diagnosed anxiety disorder, or are on any place in between on the fear scale, you have a great deal in common with me as a fellow anxiety sufferer.

I've found three key components for understanding our fear:

1. Root Cause
2. Core Catalysts
3. Situational Triggers

Root Cause

First, let's explore the *root cause*—the origin of the problem. This is the answer to questions like "What's different about me that would allow this type of fear to be present in my life?" and "Why do I struggle with fear more than other people do?"

To discuss this subject, we must tread on the sacred ground of "nature vs. nurture," the age-old debate regarding which has more influence:

- the genetic factor—the internal—what you were born with
- the environmental factor—the external—caused by your surroundings

Brilliant minds are on both sides of this subject, and people are deeply entrenched in their beliefs and their opinions. My personal experience leads me to answer that the origins of living in fear are both genetic *and* environmental. However, I believe the *root cause* of all our serious and intense fear situations (for example, chronic issues, disorders, and distortions) is genetics. I think those of us who struggle with anxiety have a physical anomaly baked within our DNA that leaves us broken in our ability to deal with fear.

Accepting a genetic basis for fear can eliminate the shame that is so often associated with our condition. We can stop asking, "What did I do wrong to cause this?"—a question that can foster a victim mentality. And no rational or reasonable person would hold someone with cerebral palsy or Down syndrome responsible for being born with the condition. We should not shame ourselves because we were born broken in this area.

People often ask me why, instead of being embarrassed, I'm so confident when I talk about my condition. The short answer is that my identity isn't wrapped up in what's wrong with me. Not only is my panic disorder not the sum total of who I am, but I didn't do anything wrong to deserve or receive it.

We are all much more than our dysfunction! My identity, as well as yours, is not centered in the fear. We have *all* been born into a fallen world with inherent flaws in our DNA. We have been born into difficulty. That's not on me, and it is not on you. What we do with it certainly is, though!

With that foundation laid for us, let's take a look at core catalysts.

Core Catalysts

Core catalyst is the term used for what launched our patterns of fear, building on our genetic disposition. This is the answer to questions like "Why is my specific situation different from others who deal with fear?" and "What happened that caused fear to manifest in me?"

In addition to believing the root cause of anxiety to be genetic, I think the difference in whether that root is awakened is environmental. I assume millions of people in this world have the very same alteration of their DNA you and I have, but theirs has never been ignited by their surroundings or life situations. The question raised, then, is "What happened in my life to start all this?" Or as I like to say, "What released the Kracken?"[2]

Think of it this way: while many people have the fuse, not everyone's will be lit.

Here are a few possible core catalysts, offered with examples.

Childhood Trauma / Early Environmental Factors

When crucial and fundamental building blocks are missing from one's childhood foundation, it can affect that child's ability to trust and to feel secure, protected, and loved. Whether environmental factors (such as homelessness, lack of food, or poverty) or trauma (such as abuse, neglect, or violence) are at play, the result can be fear manifested in an adult's life. Some people do not recall a childhood trauma because they have blocked it out, and stories of how intense counseling caused people to recall a traumatic incident in their childhoods are numerous. This process can bring some form of healing, because the catalyst has now been exposed and brought into the light—just as a murder is more easily solved when a motive is uncovered.

Distorted Worldviews and Perceptions of Reality

Many today have unhealthy views of how the world works, who they are, and how to relate to their surroundings. Consider this analogy: What if a person's home had only the "fun house" mirrors found in amusement parks so that every mirror reflected only a distorted image? Life events, especially in childhood and the teen years, can create such a perspective.

Two distortions rampant in our country are about love and marriage. So many of us have grown up in divorced homes and learned to question commitment and care between a man and a woman, forever altering how we see the world and making room for fear to creep in. The divorce of my parents when I was seven was a tremendous catalyst for my fear manifesting in my life.

In addition, the tension between a person's perception of reality and his or her worldview can create rifts that spark anxiety. Those with a religious worldview deal with additional issues like God/Satan, right/wrong, good/bad, and sin/righteousness, which can heighten the intensity.

Here are a few examples of this tension:

General (Anyone)

- Realizing that doctors do routine surgeries every day all day and that anesthesiologists put people under ten times a day all week, yet being freaked out about going into surgery for something as simple as a tonsillectomy or hernia surgery.
- Knowing your spouse is trustworthy, but still being paranoid if he or she is out late because you think an affair might be the reason.

General (Christian)

- Knowing you are an adopted child of God and that He sent His Son to die for you, yet feeling abandoned and alone.
- Knowing God's extravagant grace, but yelling at someone for failing to meet your expectations.

Personal (Mine)

- Understanding that I was just an average young boy no one thought twice about, yet feeling as though the whole world were on my shoulders or that people were out to get me.

- Preaching about the peace that passes understanding *and* that guards our hearts and minds while having a panic attack.

High-Functioning Minds

People with high-functioning minds often look at life through telescopes and microscopes, so to speak, rather than their own set of eyes. Their minds are constantly scanning the horizon for potential trouble or looking at a situation in far too much detail and finding microscopic issues. Of course, a high-functioning mind can be a blessing, like a super-fast hard drive on a computer, but there's also the potential for an imbalanced view of life. Just because we have the ability to input info doesn't mean we should.

Some examples of a high-functioning mind at work:

- Walking into a meeting or gathering with a new group of people and attempting to read everyone's personalities, sizing up their intentions and thoughts.
- Having a casual conversation with a friend, but all the while wondering if that friend is about to spring a problem or issue on you.
- Mapping out how the entire day will likely play out when it is only 8:30 a.m.

Overly Sensitive Personalities

Some personalities are far more sensitive to their environments and the people around them than others. To be a people pleaser in a world where the vast majority is rarely pleased is challenging. These sensitive types may find themselves particularly influenced by media—whether informational, entertainment, or advertising—which can easily influence or corrupt their perceptions.

Here are a few examples of being overly sensitive:

- You are the kid who has stomachaches going to school, because you are aware that bad things happen to good people in a broken world.
- You're nervous about others' perceptions of you, because you know full well not everyone operates on grace and that people can be harsh and judgmental.
- You frequently play the what-if game, using a deadly combination of your imagination and intelligence.
- You have a heightened sense of how people aren't getting along in a room and worry because you know rifts can go too far and break relationships (for example, being fearful of parents divorcing every time they fight).
- You watch a TV program and think those bad guys are really out there.
- You read a book about diseases and think you have *all* of them.
- You often run a quick assessment of risk, refusing to do something (like jump off a rock into the river) because there's at least a 3 percent chance of harm.
- You overthink and overreact on the tiniest of possibilities, as if all options are equal.

Physical Health Issues

God created us uniquely, and some of our core catalysts can be physical in nature and remedied rather easily. Historically, many conditions that were deemed "plagues of the mind" were, in fact, physical abnormalities that could be handled by practical means. Diet, vitamin/nutrient deficiencies, chemical imbalances, our nervous and endocrine systems, or other internal functions can certainly affect our minds and viewpoints. Undetected severe food allergies or a dramatic decrease in serotonin are examples of physical issues that can bring on anxiety and other emotional instabilities.

Unhealthy Rhythms of Modern Life

Few would disagree that anxiety has increased in our society in the last century like never before. Why? The pace of life for most people in our culture is unsustainable and is likely causing systemic shutdown for many. In short, we are on the road to burnout.

For example, the news frequently reports cases of road rage. This relatively new societal confrontation has two consistent factors. First, the incident is based in anxiety, resulting in anger. Second, the incident is rarely about the actual traffic situation. The driver got into the car in some state of upset and the circumstance was the match that lit the fuse already in place by way of an anxious life.

Taking vacations and days off, as well as downtime, is now often viewed as some sort of corporate weakness. "Burning the candle at both ends" seems to be an admirable and expected trait of the driven. This mind-set fuels anxiety.

Our addiction to digital devices feeds bad news and judgment from all over the world to us all day, every day. We stay in information overload mode 24/7.

How much of the anxiety issues in our society could be

eliminated if we would simply slow down, take a break, and find some peace?

Spiritual Warfare

Though some people consider it controversial, spiritual warfare is still a fact of spiritual life. If we believe in God and the Bible, then we have to believe in the Enemy, who will do anything in his power to bully us and tear us down. You might have noticed by now that the Devil and his team certainly enjoy making people's lives worse. We'll deal more with this topic in chapter 12.

The beautiful thing about discerning your core catalysts is that you can devise a battle plan specifically for your situation. If you don't know the core catalyst for your fear, how will you know where to look for answers? For example, if the core catalyst is childhood trauma, you would likely begin your process of healing in the counseling room. If the core catalyst is physical, you would sort it out in the doctor's office. If it's spiritual warfare, then the battle is fought on your knees in prayer and with fellow believers.

I believe, if diagnosed appropriately, a great number of core catalysts can be completely removed or restored. Unfortunately, for some of us, the catalyst remains a mystery, and we are still wrestling with why this condition is in our lives. However, our fear can be compensated for, worked with, and managed. The more educated we are on our catalysts, the more we may be able to identify, decrease, and eliminate them.

Situational Triggers

Situational triggers focus on what's happening today that provokes our anxiety. This component answers questions like, "Why am I so freaked out at this moment? I was fine yesterday, even an hour ago, but now I'm a mess. What's going on?" or "What is different about today? What's going on in the world around me, or within the internal world of my perspective, that is causing me to freak out?"

Triggers are where most of our day-to-day difficulties start, but they are also where we can get the most traction to overcome our condition. This is also the area where we carry the most responsibility and accountability. We might not be at fault for the root cause or core catalysts, but we are certainly in charge of how we live and what we allow to shape and influence us today. Our influences, health habits, jobs, friends, current perspectives, and daily mind-sets, all of which we may be able to control or manage, fit in this discussion.

Here are some questions to answer in making progress on identifying and managing your triggers:

Does any aspect of the calendar or clock adversely affect you? For example, perhaps your triggers regularly occur before 10:00 a.m. or always late at night. Consider analyzing the stress flow of any given time period, such as the company quotas creating more anxiety as you get closer to the end of the month. Or maybe for a parent the holidays or end-of-school craziness with activities are triggers. Many people who suffer from anxiety might never realize there is a distinct daily, weekly, monthly, or even annual pattern to their onsets.

Does a specific person or group of people adversely affect you? For example, is your anxiety triggered anytime a certain relative comes into town to visit, or the semiannual auditor shows up, or that person corners you to discuss politics again?

Does a specific situation consistently adversely affect you? A dead-stop traffic jam on the freeway, a discussion about money with your spouse, a recurring behavioral problem with a child, or a production meeting at work are all examples of possible triggers.

Identifying a pattern or recurring situation can help you navigate your triggers. You might be able to avoid some situations altogether, though that would be impossible with others. Knowing something or someone triggers you, however, can help put a plan in place to minimize or buffer the anxiety.

After you identify as many triggers as you can, think through possible solutions or ways to help yourself in those settings.

- Can you take another route to work during high traffic times?
- Is there a more comfortable place for you to sit during the staff meeting?
- Can you walk outside and get some air during your peak trigger times?
- During your overload seasons at work, can you talk to your spouse or a friend more, or even see your counselor more frequently?

So . . .

- Identify your triggers.

- Indicate patterns.
- Implement a plan.

You might be amazed at how taking stock of your life and exploring potential solutions can change the frequency of the triggers that bring your onsets of fear, anxiety, and panic.

DEFINING TERMS

When someone uses words like *stressed, anxious, worried, fearful,* and *panicked,* others can make assumptions. Connotations leave a wide gamut for interpreting these words. Let's break them down and clarify their meaning to be sure we're on the same page.

Although I've written from the perspective of the more extreme side of the pendulum—actual panic disorder—fear is the common denominator. Maybe you have experienced only one panic attack, but it was sufficient to wake you up to the need for help. Maybe you come from a family of chronic worriers and want to break the chain in your generation. Fear is fear. The only variable is the degree to which it impacts us.

To make this simple, I will discuss how I use five common terms: *worry, stress, fear, anxiety,* and *panic.*

Worry and *stress* are both general concerns toward life issues.

Fear is being afraid of something—regardless of what it is or if it is real or imaginary.

Anxiety and *panic* are both involuntary responses that come from the depths of your being and produce a sense of dread that is irrational and undetectable in its origin.

Worry, stress, and fear are common experiences that everyone has, and anxiety and panic are more specific, rare, and linked to disorders.

Because there's so much confusion and judgment about panic attacks and anxiety disorders, I want to explain again that when we talk about these, we are referring to a fear that uncontrollably rises up within us that doesn't match our current situation. We could be doing everything right, and an attack might come on anyway. We might, for instance, be in the middle of prayer or a worship service and be overwhelmed by a fear of crowds.

Don't get me wrong. Practical fear is bothersome, and we all need to deal with that too. But I'm defining panic disorder as something less controllable and often unpredictable. Usually the core catalyst is a mystery, and the solution is equally elusive. Most of the time we don't even know what we are freaking out about. With common worry, fear, and stress, we know exactly what we are concerned about.

The fear that comes with a panic attack is akin to the fight-or-flight response. If I jumped out and scared you, then rebuked you for getting scared, there would be something wrong with me—not you. If I took a swing at your face and blamed you for blinking, you would think I was crazy. Instinctual responses are common to us all and can be influenced, though not fully controlled. Yet anxiety disorders might be even more complicated than instinct. They might also be chemical. To blame a child for a chemical response to a situation would be like chastising someone for falling asleep under anesthesia. How absurd would that be?

If you lay your hand on a hot stove and your brain screams,

Move your hand, you idiot! you don't take the time to consider the implications; you instinctively pull away. When you are having a panic attack, a similar process occurs. You feel as though something terrible is going to happen and you have to get away immediately, but sometimes—most times—you can't. And forget the environment; you certainly can't escape from yourself!

The average person can be afraid, but rational thought brings him or her back to reason. Not so for those of us with anxiety disorders. For us the fear goes relatively unchecked through our systems, grabs us in a chokehold, and won't let up. This sensation is usually grounded in a perceived lack of control, being forced to do something we don't want to do, or being scared of bodily and emotional harm. Fear is a terribly brutal king who rules with an iron fist.

Let me cite some examples:

If I'm worried about something, I might be concerned to the degree that the problem takes over my thought life and leads to physical and emotional results, such as stomachaches, butterflies, hand-wringing, fretting, or distraction. This physical and mental state is where we get the phrase *worried sick.* But if I am having an anxiety or panic attack, my heart might race uncontrollably. I might feel as though I'm going to collapse, vomit, or go insane. I might experience abject fear, terror, or dread. I might even feel as though I am going to die.

I think we are all clear on the causes for normal worry, even intense stress. Some examples would be thoughts like these:

- *Will my baby die from his disease?*
- *Will I get fired and not be able to provide for my family?*
- *Will my spouse divorce me?*

Usually normal worry and stress are situational and can be tied to a specific event. But what makes anxiety problems so difficult to pin down is that they are either an improper bodily response to a normal trigger (situational) or seemingly disconnected to what's happening around us (chronic).

If someone is nervous and feels nauseated at the thought of giving an upcoming speech in a college class, this is considered normal—and understandable. If that same student is in the fetal position in the bathroom, saying, "I can't breathe" over and over again, we have a different situation.

If someone is concerned about their recent diagnosis of cancer, we think they are properly attuned to their situation. If a person is completely healthy and yet can barely focus on what other people are saying because for no apparent reason he is certain he is dying, we're talking about something else entirely.

SHARING FEAR, SHARING LIFE

You are not alone in your struggle. Consider these statistics from the Anxiety and Depression Association of America (ADAA):

- Forty million adults in the United States age eighteen and older (18 percent of the US population) are affected by anxiety disorders, the most common mental illness in the United States.
- Anxiety disorders cost the United States more than $42 billion a year, nearly one-third of the $148 billion spent on mental health.

- Generalized anxiety disorder (GAD) affects 6.8 million adults. Women are twice as likely to be affected as men.
- Six million suffer from panic disorder.
- Fifteen million have social anxiety disorder.
- Nineteen million have specific phobias.
- More than two million live with obsessive compulsive disorder (OCD), and nearly eight million live with post-traumatic stress disorder (PTSD). (Rape is the most common trigger for PTSD, not combat duty.)
- Anxiety disorder sufferers are three to five times more likely to see a doctor and six times more likely to be hospitalized than the general public.
- Thirty-six percent of those who suffer from social anxiety disorder experience symptoms for more than ten years before seeking professional help.
- Nearly one-half of those who are diagnosed with depression are also diagnosed with an anxiety disorder.[3]

The very nature of anxiety leads to isolation. Most people do not understand what is happening to us and cannot relate, no matter how much they care. Because the wound is internal, there is no obvious sign of our handicap, so we don't get much sympathy. If we were in wheelchairs, people would allow for our frailties, but because we usually look fine, the sensitivity drains away quickly. It's hard to explain to someone that even if the fear is imaginary, the physical symptoms are real. And if our condition is chronic or long-term, we may find that other people cannot sustain an emergency state of mind for that long and need to move on.

Let's face it—this fear thing is tough on our friends. It's

hard to pray for the same thing over and over, especially when it's someone else's problem.

Unfortunately, sometimes we overload one friend by dumping all our fears and pains on that one person, who melts down under the weight—and then we have no one. These days, friends are hard to come by in the first place. Because so many of us are distracted by trying to keep our own stuff together, we certainly don't have much margin left for helping anyone else with their problems. We are too overloaded ourselves. We can't blame our friends for being sick and tired of us being sick and tired when we feel the exact same way.

I know it's difficult, but believe me when I tell you, it's absolutely crucial that you have friends and a support system to walk with you through life. I know you don't want to have to explain yourself over and over again to people who don't fully understand. I know friends are hard to make and even harder to keep, but it's worth the effort. Even aside from the biblical mandates to be in community and the fact that you and I were designed to live in relationship with others, it's better to do life with friends and loved ones around us.

The truth is that people are far more understanding than we tend to give them credit for. Sure, they can't take all the weight of our fear at once or for too long, but they can handle it in appropriate doses, especially if you try for a healthy give-and-take. Remember, if people truly know your need, they can be praying for you, and praying gets Christian friends involved in fighting the battle with you. Then when they see God break through in your life, they are right there rejoicing with you and cheering you on. Church is so important, if for no other reason than getting out of your own head and allowing someone else's thoughts and perspectives to be the focus.

While my goal is to help you understand that you are not alone, I am obviously not physically in your life. It is my hope that you are not dealing with your fear by yourself. To walk this road is already brutal, but to walk without support is unthinkable. My wife intimately knows what I go through. My parents, siblings, and friends have been educated about my condition. I go through seasons with a paid professional walking me through hard times. As a pastor, I have an intercessory prayer team that prays and fasts for me, that knows me well and lifts me up daily. And yet, *I* am still the one battling this invisible foe.

Who is on your team? Who is walking with you? If you can name names, great! Hang on to and cherish those folks. Take care of them whenever you can. If you are alone, if the only help you get from this book is a determination to seek help, my goal will have been accomplished.

Other people who freak out might be closer to us than we think. One time a buddy of mine came to pick me up in his truck because we were going out of town together. I thought it was odd that he didn't even suggest we take my car. Only later did I learn that he, too, fought anxiety and panic attacks, and one of his ways of managing them was to be the driver.

There are hundreds of little tricks like that to navigate life while God is healing us. People whose anxiety is triggered by crowds tend to sit near a door or on an aisle. People with terrible hypochondria avoid online medical websites. We can all compensate to some degree. Instead of allowing the fear to trap you at home and ruin your ability to go out with friends and family, try to manage your way through by keeping a certain amount of control in the situation so you feel more peaceful.

The more we are able to compensate and make healthy choices, the more we are freed to live our lives. Hundreds of thousands of successful and productive people in the world today live with the same troubles we face. As a matter of fact, many famous people have walked the same path:

- Poet Alfred Tennyson (1809–1892) struggled with perpetual panic.
- Psychoanalysis founder Sigmund Freud (1856–1939) had a panic disorder.
- Inventor Nikola Tesla (1856–1943) experienced panic attacks and phobias.
- Physicist and mathematician Sir Isaac Newton (1642–1727) had a nervous breakdown.
- American poet Emily Dickinson (1830–1886) dealt with chronic terror.
- Scottish poet Robert Burns (1759–1796) was diagnosed with a "nervous disease."
- President Abraham Lincoln (1809–1865) had anxiety and a phobia of death.
- Irish poet William Butler Yeats (1865–1939) struggled with constant fear.
- American writer John Steinbeck (1902–1968) experienced intense anxiety and deep depression.
- In recent times, celebrities who have talked openly about their panic attacks and bouts with fear include actors Johnny Depp, Emma Stone, Scarlett Johansson,

and British pop singers Adele and Ellie Goulding, to name only a few.

Many sufferers have fought through to greatness in the midst of their difficult challenges. I hope we follow their lead of never letting our challenges shut us down.

As I hope you can see, anxiety and panic disorders are far more common than you might have thought. We are certainly not alone. Struggling with fear does not make you a bad person, a bad Christian, or a second-class citizen. It just means you have something you need to wrestle with in life.

I don't know all the reasons we suffer as we do or why life has to be so hard, but honestly, we need to realize that broken people are everywhere we look. Everyone you meet has a story to tell about their personal difficulties. It could be dyslexia, infertility, chronic fatigue, or disease and many of these challenges can be lifelong. We just happen to carry a burden less diagnosed and less understood, but those unknowns can't be our excuse to lie down and give up.

We can do this!

We can fight the fear we share.

CHAPTER 5

FLYING THROUGH FEAR: A CASE STUDY

Horror and panic themselves are forms of
violence, and diminishing them, restricting
their dimensions, is itself a civilizing act.
—Walter Kirn, novelist[1]

In spring 2002—just seven months after 9/11—I was wrapping up a study tour through Turkey and Greece, following the apostle Paul's footsteps on his missionary journeys. The United States was still on high alert, as were Americans traveling abroad, and airlines were enacting new safeguards in response to terrorist events.

In sharing this story, I will intentionally be vague about some of the details regarding the person I focus on. The emphasis should not be on the ethnicity or religion of this person, but on my own response to fear. My goal is to illustrate the level of irrationality and other negative thoughts that unbridled fear can lead us to believe is reality—when it is not.

—

The night before we left Greece, we had to set our alarms for 4:00 a.m. so we could meet the buses taking us to the airport in Athens. After an exhausting tour, getting up that early was rough. I had damaged one of my contact lenses the day before, and it had scratched my eye. This irritation was going to make a tiring trip more unpleasant. I had also run out of my anxiety meds. Super tired, missing home, scheduled to travel the final leg alone, irritated eyes, and no meds: this situation had the makings of the perfect storm.

Up to this point in my life, flying was a time to chill out, catch up on reading, creatively try to fit my six-foot-three frame into a seat built for a horse jockey, and generally zone out. While the terrorist concerns in post–9/11 days were prevalent, they were magnified on this Easter morning—a Christian holiday. Flights to the United States from abroad were on especially high alert. That really wasn't bothering me—that is, until we got to Chicago for my final leg home alone.

By this point, I was truly exhausted. The flight from Athens to Chicago had been super long. My fatigue was taking its toll, my eyes were hurting, and my lack of meds started pinging my emotional triggers. I was still far from home and, in general, irritable and anxious. But O'Hare to Sacramento was only about a six-hour trip and then I would be back with my wife and baby girl. I missed them terribly and wanted to be in my own bed.

Then *he* walked onto the plane.

The man was bald with a sizeable beard. His T-shirt had Arabic script emblazoned on it. He was also carrying an attaché case. My eyes followed him as he slid into the seat to my left, right across the narrow aisle from me.

A bit nervous about takeoffs and touchdowns, I did what I usually did: closed my eyes and drifted in my thoughts, occasionally dropping a prayer or two about angels being under the wings.

As we taxied out to the runway, my eyes popped open at the sudden sound of chanting. The bearded man had taken out his religious book of choice and was rocking back and forth with his face buried inside, praying at a slightly above normal volume. Needless to say, he captured the attention of *everyone* on the plane. Five rows up, some young man blurted out, "Oh, you've got to be kiddin'," loud enough for everyone to hear. Honestly, I agreed.

The poor guy could have been afraid to fly, or maybe it was just the designated time of day for prayer. Maybe he was praying for a safe flight for all of us. But I can tell you that no one on that flight was thinking such rational thoughts at that moment. I felt a surge of adrenaline as my anxiety began to ramp up. I couldn't possibly ignore this display, seated right next to me.

My mind began to race. What could I do? What should I do? America is a free country. This gentleman had every right to pray in his own manner in a public setting. Prayer is a precious privilege, and I respect it. I knew all of these things on a rational level, but my irrational side started to take hold— and win.

I was going through every scenario of possible doom when he suddenly stopped, put away his book, opened his attaché, and pulled out his laptop. He opened it up on the tray table and gathered a stack of small papers. Did I relax at that point, take a deep breath, and fall asleep? No. Not on your life. I might have looked as though I were resting, but I was continually darting my eyes over to what he was doing. I was now shifting into full-on paranoia.

Out of the corner of my eye, I caught a glimpse of the information on the papers. Each had a series of numbers on them that he was typing into the laptop. I could see the word *Islamic*, but that was about all I could make out. Any normal person would have let this poor man go on about his work, but I had seen far too many Jason Bourne movies to let it go. By now, I had worked the narrative into one in which the man was a radical extremist typing in secret codes for nefarious purposes. I continued to try to discern what type of world domination plan this was, but I couldn't figure it out. For the next hour, he quietly worked away while I planned my funeral.

Every five minutes or so, a healthy thought would push its way into my head about how I could be misunderstanding everything. I would quickly shove it back and continue to panic.

Just then, the flight attendant announced that it was time for lunch. When the flight attendant got to my Islamic seatmate, he told her, "I had a vegetarian meal." She asked his name, and he gave it to her. She took out her list of passengers and asked for his name again. He politely repeated it, and she looked again. And then she said something I'll never forget: "I'm sorry, sir. I'm just not seeing you on the manifest."

My thoughts screamed, *Wait! What? Not on the manifest? Are you kidding me?!* Every good Hollywood-trained spy knows the manifest is the list of passengers approved to be on the plane. Additionally, we know it's rare for someone to *not* be listed on the manifest when he or she is clearly taking up a seat. Those of us able to take it one level further might surmise that if he is not on the manifest and he is not supposed to be on the plane, then he clearly is up to no good. It was only a matter of time before the chaos would break loose.

Suddenly my semi-food lost whatever taste it had. Deeper into the world of fight-or-flight I went.

Over the next hour, my stomach churned everything I had eaten into pure acid. I was too proud to out and out panic, but make no mistake—I was freaking out.

I wanted to warn the people a few rows ahead of me that a hostage crisis was about to take place. I wanted to run to the pilot and tell him a great menace was in row 17 (not me, *him*). I wanted to curl up in a ball and hold my blankie. But I did none of that. If anyone was watching me, they saw nothing but cool—a young man just chillin' in his seat, eager to see his family and mastering some crossword puzzles.

I stayed in that mode through the next forty-five minutes. Just as I began to distract myself and calm down a bit, the man quickly scooped up his papers, slammed the laptop shut, and raised his hand to signal the flight attendant. Back on high alert once again, I eavesdropped on their conversation, which went something like this:

"Yes, sir, do you need something?"

"Yeah, I need to plug my laptop into the plane. I need to charge it."

"Well, we do have an outlet in the back, but it's a special type so I don't think it will work for you."

"It'll work." He said this flatly and confidently.

"Okay, follow me."

And he got up to go to the back of the plane, following the flight attendant.

This was it. This was the moment. He was going to take the crew hostage or blow out the door—I was sure of it. I saw no evidence of an air marshal on board (as though I would know if I saw one), so I began running through any scenario that would keep me alive and, if possible, save the lives of those on board with me. I had to admit that even in abject fear, I was still a pretty nice guy.

They had been gone only a short time when he came back alone and sat down. Either the takeover was extremely quiet or he was just setting up the next step in commandeering the plane.

After fifteen minutes of panic, my body reminded me that I really, really needed to use the restroom. I decided that if I did not feel better after visiting the lavatory, I was going to do something about this situation once and for all.

In the tiny washroom, I went through the pros and cons of causing enough trouble to force the pilot to land the plane. Sure, I would go to jail, but at least the passengers would be safe. I would take one for the team. No, I might not see my little baby grow up, but at least I would probably see her graduate.

In the end, I couldn't commit to such a rash and extreme plan, but I did decide that I would talk to the flight attendants. If I felt they weren't helpful, I might need to take my plan to the next level (although I wasn't yet certain what that would look like).

As I exited the restroom, two of the attendants were in the galley, working on drinks for passengers. I said, "Excuse me, ladies, I don't mean to bother you, but I have a question for you . . . and a concern."

"Is it about the Arabic man next to you?" one asked.

"Yeah."

"We are aware of him and we're keeping an eye out, but he really hasn't done anything to be of concern."

I was starting to feel better already. At least they were alert and he was on their radar. My stomach started to settle a bit. But then the other flight attendant chimed in, "Ya know, I had friends on those flights that crashed into the towers. The way I see it, when it's your time to go, it's your time to go."

My mind screamed, *No! Stop talking! You aren't helping!*

The first flight attendant spoke again. "We have had some threats today internationally, and we are on alert. However, on 9/11, the planes involved were much bigger than ours, and the assailants were in pairs. As far as we can tell, this man is alone and has done nothing to indicate he is any kind of threat. If anything significant comes up, I will notify the pilot."

I thanked them profusely and headed back to my seat. Now there were only a few hours left until we reached Sacramento. Surely I could hang on until then. I went back into my quasi-prayer-but-I'm-just-scared mode. I determined there was nothing I could do at that point. Actually, there was nothing I *should* have done at that point. I kept asking myself, *What would a rational person do?*—a question I have had to ask myself far too many times. I agreed with the tiny voice inside that told me to relax and let God take care of this. After all, anything I did would only complicate matters and make a bad situation out of what was still not even an actual crisis. Tense, but somewhat settled, I went back to my crossword puzzle.

Finally the pilot announced we were approaching Sacramento and told us to stow our electronics for the crew to prepare for landing. *What a relief,* I thought. *I'm almost home.* And that's when he, once again, took out his book of religion and started chanting prayers. My fellow travelers visibly tensed up, and I went for one final round of survival as the plane started to descend.

Even after touching down, deplaning, going to baggage claim, and getting to the car, I was still shaken. I barely kissed my wife, but after driving away, telling her a bit of the story, and getting some American fast food in me, I did feel the world was right again.

—

Here is the worst part about this story: I have been afraid to fly ever since, which is really, really inconvenient. I still fly, but I'm miserable. For whatever reason, that experience triggered something in my psyche that tells me flying is unsafe. No matter how much I logically try to replace those thoughts, my mind has firmly etched this new fear into my anxiety repertoire.

Because of my distorted sense of humor, my favorite people to tell about my fear of flying are Christian pilots. The smiles on their faces are priceless. They look like they are staring at a five-year-old child. Only a few have stooped low enough to point out the obvious with the question, "You do realize you were less safe driving to the airport than actually being on a flight, right?" Only one has dropped the line, "C'mon, man, where is your faith? God knows how to fly!"

"I know, I know!" I say. "But that's what irrational fear is all about—it's irrational!"

The whole story I just told you is full of irrationality. Profiling that poor, sweet, innocent, friendly man; considering causing a disturbance to get a completely secure plane to land just so I could feel safe; entertaining spy-fantasy absurdity—it was all ridiculous and embarrassing. My reactions were way out of line.

Think about the last time you dealt with a circumstance like this. Taking a hard look at the common reactions we have when we're afraid can help us avoid embarrassment (or possible jail time) as well as better navigate and possibly evade future dilemmas.

WE FAIL TO ASSESS

When we go into a potentially stressful setting, such as the one I was in on the flight, we must assess the situation ahead of time and plan on buffering ourselves from our stressors as much as possible. Work to avoid obvious issues, such as running out of medication, and allow for exhaustion. Taking a moment to assess is also important if you find yourself unexpectedly confronted with fear. In my situation, the flight was not full; what if I had simply and quietly requested to move to another seat and gone to sleep? Assessing is far easier in hindsight, but the more we learn to watch and allow for predictable factors going *into* a situation, the better we can successfully navigate our way *away from* anxiety.

WE MAKE FALSE ASSUMPTIONS

Stereotyping and profiling are types of assumption. I was certainly guilty of both when I focused solely on the man's appearance and actions. I coupled the recent events of 9/11 with his nationality and religion, making damaging assumptions. He didn't suffer as a result of my suspicions, but I certainly did. Making assumptions about people and situations before getting the facts usually gets us into trouble. Minimizing rash judgments and relying on rational logic could save us from many bouts of fear.

WE GIVE IN TO PARANOIA

While paranoia is certainly a symptom of actual mental illness, we all can let our minds get the better of us by contemplating situations that do not truly exist. For children, fear can create a boogeyman in the closet; for adults, it can turn into the looming doom of financial crises, marital issues, and personal meltdowns we believe are on the horizon. We can jump to conclusions in a heartbeat, imagining catastrophes that will never actually take place. It's important that we refuse to let our minds simply wander or concoct fairytales. We are in charge. We must corral our negative thoughts before they take hold.

WE DEVELOP AN US-AGAINST-THEM MIND-SET

While this reaction is a by-product of assumption and paranoia, I want to draw attention to how we set ourselves up against those we identify as different. We look at people and draw lines between them and us, making perceived enemies or at least suspects. The moment we make those decisions, we set up a defense, which then enacts fear and anxiety. After all, what do our minds and bodies do in the presence of a perceived threat? What if only *real* threats were threats to us? Our fear would have less opportunity to manifest itself.

WE INDULGE IN FANTASY

Our pervasive and intrusive media, coupled with our Western civilization mind-sets, can create a blurred line between reality and fantasy. Using a very real man seated next to me, I created a suspense movie in my own mind for an entire flight. What if I had disciplined myself to stay in reality and had not allowed myself to write the Hollywood script in my head?

WE ALLOW FEAR TO ESCALATE

This story is a rising tide of escalation, from the moment the man sat down to the moment I drove away from the airport. I took myself on the crazy ride; that other passenger had nothing to do with what I created out of my fear. How many situations could we thwart if we realized we were escalating our fears, got a grip, and came back down to reality?

WE FOCUS TOO MUCH ON OURSELVES

On the plane, who was I constantly thinking about? While I thought I was focusing on the man, I actually was focusing on me. *My* safety. *My* life. *My* well-being. As Christ constantly taught us, focusing on others keeps us balanced. Is it possible I could have struck up a conversation and made a friend with the man across the aisle? Maybe not, but I will never know. Why? Because I was self-focused.

WE CLING TO CONTROL

We have a love-hate relationship with control. On that flight, I felt out of control of the situation, my own safety, and my own mind—but the harder I worked to devise a plan to take command, the more helpless I felt. This kind of helplessness typically brings some level of fear, but for those of us trying to cope with anxiety and panic, grabbing the wheel of an out-of-control vehicle brings on a wreck. As a Christian, I am to constantly be releasing control from my hands and giving it to God. The beautiful reality of handing things over to God is that we are trusting in someone to handle our situation who is far more capable than we are.

I am certainly not saying that applying any of these suggestions is easy, but the more we consider alternatives to freaking
out, and the better we get to know ourselves, the more that
education can help us.

Despite my use of humor, sharing the deepest and darkest
mental and emotional chaos I experienced on that flight is not
fun for me. I'm not proud of those moments. But, as with many
situations I share in these pages, I divulge them to be honest
and, ultimately, to help you learn more about your fear. I'm bet-
ting you have a story or two of your own to rival mine. You
likely got halfway into this particular account and thought, *Oh,
this reminds me of the time I* . . . The more we share, look into,
get honest about, and learn from these situations, the better we
can be. Help and hope—remember? I hope you will consider a
few of your own stories and look for signs of the eight destructive behaviors above. Ask yourself the following questions:

- How can I better assess situations before I get into
  trouble?
- What assumptions that lead to fear and anxiety do I
  tend to make about people and circumstances? Are
  there patterns I can detect and avoid?
- What settings tend to tempt me to move from reality
  to paranoia? How can I avoid making that jump?
- In what circumstances do I create an us-against-them
  mind-set? At home, at church, at work, with friends?
  When interacting with people of a different race,
  ethnicity, religion, or economic class than mine?
- Where do I tend to blur the lines of reality and fantasy,
  taking myself to an unhealthy place?

- When I start to fear or feel anxious, in what ways am I escalating my own panic? Are there any steps I can take in recurring situations to de-escalate?
- How much is self-focus playing into my fear and anxiety? What action steps can I take to focus more on others and God? How much does control—or lack of it—dictate my fear? What can I do when I feel out of control? How can I learn to be okay when I am not in charge?

CHAPTER 6

MEDS: MAGIC OR MESS?

*There are two things panic patients hate to do. They
hate to take medication and they hate to go to doctors.*
—Earl Campbell, pro football legend[1]

Looking down the staircase I knew I was never going to make
it. If I started the descent, I would black out halfway down
and tumble the rest of the way to the concrete pavement. My
eyes simply wouldn't focus, *couldn't* focus. I didn't know why.

I knew I had been feeling "off" for several weeks at my
job as an insurance claims adjuster. In between going through
stacks and stacks of files and answering phone calls, my vision
would get blurry. I constantly felt nauseated. But today was
different. This particular day, I knew I needed to go home,
but between me and my car were *way* too many concrete and
steel stairs in my office building, and walking was something
I couldn't manage at the moment.

Why is this happening to me?

I'm only twenty-four-years old, a strong, healthy, and responsible married man.

What is going on?

I went back to my assistant manager to ask for a ride home. I thought, *Not only is she not about to let me off work, she certainly isn't going to drop everything to take me home.* But I felt I had no choice but to ask.

After a brief discussion, my assistant manager and manager determined that one of them would take me directly to my doctor's office. I was now embarrassed and humiliated. They looked at me with half concern, half irritation. I didn't blame them. I was complicating their day.

By the time I got to the doctor's office, my heart was racing and I was completely freaked out. My assistant manager sat with me in the waiting room until my wife arrived. It felt like an eternity before they called my name. I went back to see the doctor—who was just shy of Rip Van Winkle's age—and he looked me over and ran some quick tests. His diagnosis? "You're fine," he said.

Really? I feel as though I'm going to die!

I was about to argue when my wife said those now-famous words: "Doctor, do you think it could be stress?"

The ancient and wise one looked at me and said, "Well, he doesn't look stressed." Clearly he'd received his medical license online—last week.

My wife countered, "What if it's internal? Lance holds on to a lot inside."

The doctor thought for a moment and mumbled, "It's possible."

At that point, he walked over to his counter where he kept

the boxes of sample medication. He grabbed the one marked Zoloft and told me to try it.

That was in 1996.

I've been on medication ever since that day.

And I'm not the only one taking meds: In 2007, 26.8 million people received treatment for anxiety, with $36.8 billion spent on treatment—half of which was for medications.[2]

If you are an anxiety sufferer who is not on any medication, or if you are reading this book to help a loved one, I want to encourage you to continue to educate yourself in this important area. Maybe your doctor has discussed with you the possibility of taking meds and you are looking for more guidance to make as informed a decision as possible.

Many issues surround the use of medications; they can be wonderful, or they can be destructive. My goal in this chapter is to share some of my personal stories about taking medication and what I have learned.

MYTHS AND MISUNDERSTANDING

I have endured well-meaning people telling me that if I only had more faith or was a better Christian, my anxiety problems would go away. They have also made it clear that medication is not for "true" Christians, but only for the weak and faithless.

Are you kidding me? Really? Do these folks have any idea what such comments do to someone's heart? What am I supposed to do with those statements? How do I respond to such uninformed criticism?

I am a pastor by vocation, who made the career choice to

dedicate myself to serving Christ in the church. I live every day to sacrificially serve others. I pray constantly. I know the Word of God backward and forward. I lead worship services. I train people in living the Christian life. I live as if God and His Word are a reality and are as natural to me as breathing. I know of no one who feels he needs God or loves God more than I do—and yet here I am, struggling still.

Unfortunately, I am not the only one to whom people have said those ignorant and hurtful statements. The modern church culture still assigns far too much stigma to medication and has a poor understanding of mental health issues, even those as pervasive in our society as anxiety and depression.

As I mentioned previously, much of this attitude surrounds an improper biblical interpretation of the words of Christ and authors who misuse the words *anxiety, fear,* and *worry.* Rather than seeking understanding, so many Christians are stuck with an ethos of judgment for people suffering from these disorders—*especially* if they need medication. This not only alienates sufferers from the church community, but it distances us from help through intercession by others. If we are afraid to talk about these issues, then no one knows about them. And if no one knows, then no one is praying.

This simply is not right.

This ignorance is hurting far too many people and causing church members, even pastors and leaders, to hide their pain. We are driving people away from the Light, where they can find help, and forcing them to hide in the dark, trying to help themselves the best they can.

The Anxiety Centre of Alberta, Canada, noted that out of the 40 million Americans annually who will experience an impairment due to an anxiety condition, only about 13 million will receive treatment (just 33 percent)—and of those only 1.3 million will receive proper treatment (10 percent of the 33 percent). Unfortunately, they also found that those who experience anxiety and stress have a high propensity for drug abuse and addictions.[3]

Why are so few people seeking the proper help? According to their research, most encounter real and perceived barriers to help, including this attitude: "They may believe there is a stigma attached to mental illness and wish to avoid any association with it [or] they may be avoiding the perceived appearance of 'weakness.'"[4]

TO MED OR NOT TO MED

With an honest and open—yet critical—mind, let's take a moment to tackle the tough, practical questions about the use of medication.

Depending on what causes an anxiety disorder, medication can provide help. But because over-medication and needless medication is a possibility, I think *everyone* on medication must regularly ask these questions:

- Do I *need* this?
- Do I *still* need this?
- *Why* do I need this?

Because we are dynamic, ever-changing humans, periodic assessment is appropriate and wise. The question still remains, however, whether taking meds is a good solution in the first place.

Let's explore three underlying questions most often asked.

Is Medication a Crutch?

Of course it is a crutch! A person with a broken leg needs a crutch for forward motion. It's what a crutch does—gives support for an infirmity. Clearly, an uninjured person using a crutch would make us all question his lazy motives. But when we see someone with a disability using one, we fully understand the need and are grateful the person has help to move about.

The concept should be no different with medication. I find it intriguing that some of the very same critics of anxiety medication talk about their own use of various prescription and over-the-counter aids for physical ailments such as arthritis, headaches, joint pain, and back pain, citing how they can't even function without the relief.

Culturally, we have drawn lines between physical relief and mental and emotional support. The question is, why?

Is Medication Use Morally Neutral?

I do believe medications prescribed by doctors are morally neutral devices, but using them too much or for purposes other than what they're designed for is a problem. Whether an overdose is intentional or an accident, the end result is the same. When people take pain meds to excess because they can't deal with life, they become no different from a junkie on the street. If people take anxiety medications because they won't submit to learning how to wrestle through disappointments, they're sliding down an unhealthy slope.

Regardless, we should be slow to judge. We need to think about the times in our own lives when we've used different kinds of "help" to get through what we should have handled head-on. To avoid relationships, issues, and crises, people "medicate" with morally problematic substances like

- alcohol
- marijuana
- pornography
- illicit sex

and with moral neutrals such as

- the Internet
- social media
- shopping
- food

All of these avenues might be used for distractions and diversions in avoiding real life. Like prescribed medications, the items on the neutral list can be engaged in positively and constructively. Yet countless people are addicted to each item on these lists—some to several of them at one time. Regardless, to demand that people immediately drop their "drug of choice" and just "get over it" is ignorant, foolish, and mean. And let's get real—there is a strong likelihood that you have used one of these substances to medicate your personal pain.

With great medication comes great responsibility. We have a responsibility to use medication for only and exactly what the doctor prescribed it to do. There is no excuse for abusing medication or using pills to block out God and His work in us. I strongly believe in personal responsibility and not blaming everyone else for my problems. I feel we as Christians need to be held accountable for our medication use, and we need to constantly assess if we are honoring the Lord with what we take and how we are approaching the management of our fear.

Considering all these factors, I strongly believe in the value of medication as a morally neutral and beneficial option. Despite the temptations to mask the dangers of addiction, I feel the proper use of meds is a worthwhile option to pursue. For so many, anxiety disorder is absolutely debilitating. If people who suffer can be responsibly helped by the use of medication, then why should anyone be resistant?

Is Medication an Easy Way Out?

Some of us buy into the idea that taking any medication for anxiety and depression is taking the easy way out and is therefore sinful. We think we should just tough it out. But . . .

Is there benefit to our spirit by being miserable every day?

Is there benefit to being unable to go to work because our bodies won't cooperate?

Do we honor God by being unable to see straight—literally?

Do we honor God by feeling as though we are going to die?

Is that what pleases God?

Is that what this life is for?

Honestly, at this phase of life it's unlikely that I could do my job without the help of medication. I could possibly struggle through sometimes and just be miserable. But whom does that approach help? I would not be able to do my job well, counsel others, go to the hospital to pray with the sick, or preach the Word of God with power. I would have to resign from being a pastor and leave my calling. I would have to quit. Is that what God wants? Is that what the people I help need?

At this point in my life, there is no cure for me that I know of. Other than medication, there is no long-term, significant help that allows me to remain upright and healthy. I have chosen to take what is absolutely necessary and move forward in my pursuit of God—and my life.

I am certainly not offering a mandate for all believers, and I would never force the idea of medication on someone else. I want to share how *I* feel called by God to handle the uniqueness of *my* situation. Medication is a pathway I would suggest or counsel others to follow, if they feel so called, but we each must come to peace with how we handle our lives.

Here is my bottom-line statement about my own situation: *I take as little medication as I need to make it through.*

I take enough to keep alert and in control, *but* I take an amount that allows me to still feel some of the symptoms of my condition so they are a constant reminder that I need to make as many healthy life choices as possible.

I thank the Lord for medication, and I will take it as needed. Yet as the Lord heals me, I will receive that healing and adjust accordingly.

As I discover new tools and strategies that help me, I will take advantage of them, and adjust my medication as needed. But until I have freedom, I will not stop taking my meds. If I need to remain on them for the rest of my life, so be it. At the same time, I'll maintain my goal to minimize my intake, with the hope of someday being able to get off medication entirely. Why? Because I realize that medication comes with consequences.

SIDE EFFECTS

I'm not foolish enough to think that taking meds doesn't come at a cost. Just like crutches end up giving you bruises and sore arms or, if used too long, prevent full healing of an injured leg, so too there are consequences to using medications.

If you read any label of possible side effects, you would never take *anything*! Just listen to the last ten seconds of any pharmaceutical commercial. The warnings are flat-out scary. The ad usually tells you it's possible that taking medication X can make you worse, or even replace your symptoms with the exact same thing: "Take this for nausea, but a possible side effect is nausea!" In addition, unintended consequences can go along with listed side effects. For example, some medications tear down other parts of your body, such as the liver or kidneys, or they hinder other mental and emotional functions.

Honestly, I've been on the meds for so long, I don't remember what life was like before them. Is memory loss a side effect? (I can't remember.)

One of the actual side effects of my medication is sleepiness, and I often wonder how much my emotional state is affected by what I take:

- Does my medication make me *more* or *less* emotional?
- Am I as emotionally connected as I should be?

- Does the medication keep me aloof from relationships?
- Is my marriage subtly affected?
- Is my ability to listen to God impacted?
- Is my interaction with church members ever hindered?

I must continue to ask myself these questions to constantly evaluate and consider the possibilities.

As God placed Adam and Eve in the garden of Eden to be stewards, we have been given our bodies to tend. A large part of stewardship is exercising one of our God-given fruits of the Holy Spirit—self-control. I have to be a steward of my life, so I am a steward of my fear; therefore, I am a steward of my medication. I do not and will never take this responsibility lightly or flippantly. Any use of medication is about stewardship on both sides—*taking* as needed and *stopping* when not needed.

It's tempting to just live life and not check in or adjust. We get comfortable and don't want to rock the boat, but we have a responsibility to shake things up when necessary. Some of us need to get on meds, despite our discomfort, and some of us need to wean ourselves off because it's time. Both are valid considerations.

Of course, before you make *any* decisions regarding medications, talk with your doctor. Part of your stewardship is taking medications properly. Medication is a gift, so we must never abuse it. Suddenly stopping it might be downright lethal. Please always engage with medication wisely and with counsel.

A PERSONALIZED, MANAGED SOLUTION

Because each of us is unique, different medications will react differently with our systems. I have found that most of the major medications affect me in a similar fashion, but that is not the norm for most people. Most folks I know have found that each anxiety or depression medication affects them differently—sometimes in extreme ways. One might make them feel edgy, another lethargic. Another complication is how much you are taking: a high dose of some medications is dangerous, but with others, there is little difference between a higher dosage and a lower one. The point is, it can be hard to find the right medication for *you*.

We can be so exhausted from coping with freaking out that we have no patience to go through the process of finding the right medication—so we throw the whole idea out the window and try to move on. Please don't do that. If you are going to examine routes other than medication, that's great, but make sure you are doing so in a well-thought-out manner and not just reacting to the fact that the process might be challenging. Your system can take some time to adjust to a new medication, so you don't even know if it's working properly until you've made it through a miserable couple of weeks. That's difficult for most of us, but if you stick it out, there's a real possibility that you can find some much-needed relief.

Once you're on a medication, be aware that your body might go through waves and phases of anxiety that ebb and flow. It's possible that what you are taking right now will need to be adjusted down the road. Make sure you do so with the full knowledge of and advice from your doctor. When you take the prescribed steps to alter the dose, the same rules apply as when switching meds: your body might take a while to absorb the dosage and hit a groove. Make the changes in a controlled manner and allow the proper time. Watch the impact on your body.

With the advice of my doctor, I have adjusted my medications regularly. I wait until I'm on a semi-peaceful plateau for at least six months and then I adjust down, if possible. If my body reacts poorly, I get back to where I was and wait it out to see what adjustments I can make in my life to compensate.

Finally, know that your body can build up a tolerance to pretty much everything—including medication. I found that during my last major bout of anxiety, I had to change medications because higher doses of the previous one weren't working. It's possible that you could have a similar experience. You might find that one medication works for a while, but then your body builds up a tolerance and it no longer helps you. Usually this tolerance builds up over a long time, but be aware and stay alert to changes. If you are increasing dosage under your doctor's care and there's no positive change, then perhaps you are on the wrong medication. The good news is there's enough research and competition in the pharmaceutical field that we have a whole bunch of medications to choose from.

—

My deep conviction is that God has given us science and medicine as a gift to help us in our frailties. As I said before, that gift comes with great responsibility. All of God's gifts can be distorted and abused—even spiritual gifts. Let's make sure His gifts remain gifts, not curses, if we choose to take medication to support our lives and callings.

CHAPTER 7

FROM THE INSIDE OUT

The highest possible stage in moral culture is when
we recognize that we ought to control our thoughts,
—Charles Darwin, naturalist[1]

In this chapter, I have pulled together a "toolbox" of practical strategies I use to manage fear in my life. I hope some of them might be of help as you work toward managing your own fear. I would encourage you to consider each one I discuss, whether or not you feel a certain strategy will help you right now. We all have times and seasons when we deal with certain issues more than others, but then life changes and we struggle in different places. I pray these suggestions can help, heal, and bring hope to you.

PLAY MIND GAMES

Discipline Your Thoughts

We are surrounded by media that bombard us with messages—good and bad—that influence us. Unfortunately,

Wall Street and Hollywood aren't in the business of raising healthy, well-adapted people; they are in the money business. (In fact, it wasn't until I was in college that I fully accepted that even news stations are in the entertainment business and not in the information business.) We design our worldviews by what we hear, see, and interact with. What if those influences are affecting us in harmful ways?

I was raised largely by Hollywood. Well, to be fair, Hollywood *and* my mom. (Oddly, there is no greater divide than between those two. My mom hated movies, and I loved them.) My dad loved movies, too, so he and I would talk about them endlessly. But as much as movies were a bonding agent between my father and me, the messages in films and other media messed with my head. I watched enough movies, read enough books, and listened to enough music that my mind was saturated with every thought and perspective known to man.

Because I was a sensitive kid, a lot of those images, concepts, and story lines shaped and marred my view of reality. I began to think the world was as it appears in the movies. Unfortunately I focused more on the scary parts than the fun parts. I would mentally log the scripts almost as deeply as I did my own memories. Sad (but not surprising) to say, Hollywood was neither looking out for my best interests nor promoting the power and presence of the Lord.

Throughout my life I've had to unlearn a lot of what I've seen, read, and heard. I also had to surgically separate the fiction in my brain from the facts of the Bible. I had to place thoughts into their proper categories. I had to learn the discipline of saying no to some thoughts and the art of replacing them with better ones.

The difference between Peter sinking in the waves and walking on water was perspective. Who and what was he staring at? If he kept his eyes on Christ, he could do the impossible. But when he looked at the waves, he began to sink. The Bible tells us to take every thought captive to the obedience of Christ (2 Cor. 10:5) and to think on things that are true, honorable, just, pure, lovely, commendable, excellent, and worthy of praise (Phil. 4:8). The simplest takeaway from those verses would be that we can't let our minds go wherever they want to wander. We need to direct them back to what is life-giving, peaceful, and good.

Is it truly possible to direct our thoughts? Doesn't random information come into our minds, regardless of whether we want it to? Well, yes and no. We might have random stuff come in, but we don't need to let it stay there. Also, our thoughts are not quite as random as we might think. Let me give you an example.

How many times have you pondered quarks in our universe? Probably none, if you don't know what they are. How many dreams have been infused with images of deep-sea anglerfish? How many nightmares do you have about the ravages of the bubonic plague? My point is that our thoughts aren't completely random; they are a selection from our library of knowledge and experience. We will never think many thoughts because we have never been aware of the object of those thoughts.

What stocks our thought library? When we start to freak out, our minds tend to pull from the scary section. We must minimize this section of our minds as much as we possibly can.

Part of stewarding our bodies is controlling the influences

we allow to fill our minds. We are hypersensitive people with anxiety issues, so we need to be careful about what we let saturate them. We might not be able to control our panic attacks, but we can certainly remove unnecessary triggers. I'm still a movie freak, but I will not see some types of movies because I can't watch them without experiencing a negative impact. In my twenties, I read the newspaper every day to stay up on current events, but after a particularly nasty season of anxiety, I gave it up for years. Even now, I filter the news feeds I frequent online.

One of the most helpful tools I have used to discipline my thoughts is what I call "changing the channel." Simply put, this is picturing my thoughts as a TV show. When I am "viewing" something unhealthy, scary, stressful, or that I simply don't need to be dwelling on, I change the channel by picturing myself clicking an imaginary remote control. Now, as in real life, the next channel might be rough, too, so I click to the next. Almost certainly within a moment or two—or a "channel" or two—my mind shifts back to the original that was freaking me out in the first place. I must go through the process again, but this time click through enough channels that I will have a hard time getting back to the original.

I fully realize this might sound silly to some, like a ridiculous mind game, but when we suffer as we do, anything that helps is good. Something you do might sound silly to me, but, hey, when something works, take it!

Distract Yourself

In the story about my plane flight, I mentioned crossword puzzles. They are a hobby of mine. While I don't do them all the time, I enjoy them like I enjoy jigsaw puzzles—as a distraction and diversion. I'm also a fanatic about cell phone games. They get my mind out of its common fear-prone patterns and into something that can be both focused and solved. What I do for a living is open-ended with little sense of control or completion. I compensate by losing myself in something that is contained and ordered.

Psychologists have known for years that emotions come from a different part of the brain than logic and that to make that shift from one side to the other can be as difficult as complex math. When a panic attack begins, try to occupy yourself with some sort of puzzle. If you are in a meeting, jot down complicated math problems and try to solve them while you are still listening to what's going on. Just having to multitask can help you make the shift to a more logical state of mind.

To be healthy inside this disorder, our minds simply cannot be allowed to go wherever they want. We need to be in control of the content we dwell on. And because the heart of our problem is one of perspective—feeling unsafe when we are actually safe—anything we can do to alter that perspective into something healthier is going to help us, no matter what our fear has grabbed hold of.

Focus on Others

I have touched on this practical help already, but I believe getting my focus off myself has been important over the years. The more I stare at myself, the more flaws I find and the more fear I can feel. The more I analyze my body, the more my hypochondria fires up. The more I reflect on my limitations, the lower the ceiling on my abilities gets. But the more I focus on other people and outside myself, the more I shift into a problem solver who can use my tools to minister to others rather than being blinded by my own troubles.

Get your mind on other people and how you can meet their needs. When you are busy helping the people around you, loving them and crying, laughing, and praying with them, there is less time to obsess about what's wrong with you and what could possibly go wrong in the future. I'm not saying to cram your life full of activity so you don't have time to think. I am saying to direct your mind away from introspection as much as possible.

Our anxiety naturally turns our focus inward because we have alarms (real and imaginary) going off in our own minds, telling us something needs to be done—right now! A healthy refocus on real issues and other people's lives might lessen your fear, as well as open the door to healthy opportunities for ministry.

MAINTAIN BOUNDARIES: CHOOSE WHEN TO FIGHT YOUR BATTLES

Recognizing the times and places for sorting out our issues is important. Right before going to sleep is not the time to do that. I have a rule that I will not solve any pressing problem or make decisions after eight o'clock at night. I absolutely refuse. Nighttime, as it is for so many sufferers, is my most stressful time, and I am usually the most anxious in the evening "prime time" hours. By bedtime, I know I'm not thinking clearly. Any decisions I need to make, or any assessments of how life is going, must be put off until tomorrow, in the light of a new day.

I say to myself, *If I still feel this way in the morning, I might do something about it, but I'm not doing anything about it tonight.* I block out any worries as much as I possibly can. I just refuse to go there.

USE HUMOR: DON'T TAKE (MOST OF) LIFE SERIOUSLY

Mark Twain said that the human race has one really effective weapon: laughter.[2] I believe God wants us to be so peaceful that our laughter is easy and our hearts are light. Humor and laughter are important to all types of people and personalities, but for some they're as vital as oxygen. I am certainly one of those people. I can, at times, make a radical shift in direction toward humor in the midst of a rather tragic situation. Of course, I never mean to make light of pain, but to divert my own feelings away from fear and panic.

Living with anxiety is heavy with the load of fear, and that load often feels unbearable to carry. Many have been emotionally crushed under its monumental weight. But laughter lifts burdens. It's a de-stressor and a heart-lightener. Apart from the powerful physical effects brought to our bodies, laughter releases tension from the soul. We need that release to alter our perceptions and recalibrate our nerves.

No matter how God designed your personality, He created you with the ability to laugh and an inner craving to outwardly express your joy. Maybe right now life is too heavy for you to even imagine a hearty belly laugh, but hopefully as you are following along with my journey, you can chuckle just a bit in the midst of life's madness. And maybe in the midst of an oncoming storm, you can find a ray of light in the warmth of a smile.

How do you recapture the joy that fear so often steals from you? If you look at your life closely, you will see both aspects that add to joy and allow humor and those that take it away. If you are already a heavy-hearted person, or an intense person by design, you might not even realize the power of laughter in your own life. I ask you to reconsider. We all need catalysts in life that brighten our spirits and ease tension. Maybe tonight you need to watch a good comedy! Reflect for a moment on what your environment is like. Be realistic and honest with yourself.

- With whom do you spend time?
- How much pressure do you place on yourself and how much of it is necessary?
- When do you take time out to play?
- When do you allow yourself to open up your spirit and laugh? Are you able to laugh at yourself?

I live by the rule that I take God and His Word very seriously, but little else—and certainly *not* myself.

There was likely a time in the past when you laughed with a light heart, and there will be again in the future. We are cyclical beings, and life has phases and seasons. We have extra rough times and extra blessed times. I certainly know there are times it can be hard to remember the good, but we must.

EXERCISE SPIRITUAL DISCIPLINES:
SLOW DOWN AND REFLECT

In part 3, I will cover the spiritual connection to our fear in much more detail from my perspective as a pastor. But now I want to highlight some disciplines that can have a positive impact on highly strung individuals like us, starting with two that often get ignored in modern Christian teaching: silence and solitude.

A close look at the life of Jesus Christ reveals that He implemented all the healthy spiritual disciplines. He fasted. He was chaste for the Father's will. He practiced withdrawing from the crowds to be still in the Father's presence. He made sure some of those environments were entirely silent, and He controlled His own voice.

Our world is busy and loud. ("What?" you say. I said, *"Our world is busy and loud!"*) Those two atmospheric conditions have dramatic effects on our ability to think, rest, calm down, and be in touch with our spirits, minds, and bodies. Whether we go out for a walk alone in a quiet place or withdraw into a prayer closet, we need a lot more quiet and a lot more slowing down in our lives if we are going to be healthy.

Making time for reflection—especially remembering our blessings—is another way to find relief from freaking out. The book of Deuteronomy in the Bible is filled with the command to *remember.* The Jews were even commanded to hold exercises that would help them recall the good times. They set up rock piles as altars of remembrance. They wrote down war victories, miracle stories, and chronicles of blessing and hid them away to periodically bring out later. God invented feasts, celebrations, and mandatory gatherings just to celebrate God's great blessings that they might otherwise forget. Even the Lord's Supper—or Communion—we regularly take part in is because Jesus said, "Do this in remembrance of me" (Luke 22:19). It's so easy to forget the good times and what God has done for us. We must be vigilant to remember, reflect, and enjoy the blessings.

Reflection can also help us understand this truth that emerges from Scripture: God tends to allow temporary suffering for His children. When we suffer, we can easily slip into the mind-set that we will *always* suffer, but that is not true.

In the well-known Good Shepherd passage in Psalm 23, we see that we only walk "*through* the valley of the shadow of death"—we don't camp out there or live there. Daniel was in the lions' den only one day. Joseph, although imprisoned for years, was not permanently housed there but released for service to the Lord. Job's suffering was temporary, and in the end, he was blessed even more than before. When the apostle Paul wrote of the sufferings of this life in 2 Corinthians 4, he called them "light and momentary troubles" (v. 17 NIV). Even the severe judgments God leveled against northern (722 BC) and southern (586 BC) Israel, where the Israelites were defeated and taken away in captivity, were not forever; they were eventually brought back home.

We must certainly endure long-term struggles, but even if our struggles remain for our entire lives, nothing compares to the glory of the next life (Rom. 8:18).

God's goodness and care for His children are clearly shown in times of respite, sometimes in partial or total healing, and in seasons of restoration. The key is to keep our hearts in a place where we can receive and enjoy those blessings and breaks, without letting our anxiety rob us of them.

WRITE IT DOWN: KEEP A JOURNAL

Journaling is a great tool to help direct your thoughts. You might be amazed at how writing out your thoughts, hopes, and fears can help you discover what your struggle is really about. Start at the beginning of your journey with fear and write through your story, much the way I did in part 1. Try to identify what you think might be possible core catalysts that set you on this path. Make a list of the triggers that led to your tension today and of areas you might want to change to bring about a healthier lifestyle to help you in your battle.

RECEIVE COUNSELING: ACCEPT PROFESSIONAL HELP

Counseling and therapy from trusted professionals provide incredible benefits. It is so healthy to pay someone highly qualified to focus entirely on . . .

- listening deeply and intently,
- giving responsible feedback about our emotional lives,
- helping us evaluate how we are processing life,
- tracking any unhealthy thinking patterns,
- exposing inappropriate coping mechanisms, and
- retraining our mind-sets in a way we can understand.

I know pride stops many people from going to a counseling professional. If that is you, please reconsider and take advantage of this beautiful and wonderful area of expertise, training, and gifting that God has provided. A good Christian counselor who connects with you and can speak into your life is worth his or her weight in gold. My therapist is absolutely wonderful. I thank the Lord for her and what God has done through her in my life.

—

In this chapter, I have focused my energy on talking through several helps focused on our internal makeup—the inside out. In the next chapter, I move toward external helps—the outside in.

CHAPTER 8

FROM THE OUTSIDE IN

I suffer panic attacks . . . and I have become
addicted to jogging. It might sound odd
but a lot of good has come out of it.
—Ellie Goulding, pop singer[1]

Many of the triggers for anxiety have to do with our physical beings. Our bodies are like a sensitive ecosystem in which each part affects the other. It might seem odd that what we do with our physical bodies could affect the way we think, but it does. Without getting into a detailed analysis of the chemical composition of the human body, let's take a look at some "low-hanging fruit," some obvious activities we can do to help us be healthy while living with anxiety. With a few small adjustments, we can avoid potential land mines of day-to-day triggers.

EXERCISE FREQUENTLY

Exercise can both let out pent-up energy and release endorphins—neurotransmitters that produce euphoric feelings of peace, relaxation, and energy. Exercise also releases tension within muscles tightened from inactivity. When we exercise, we can expend energy so we are too tired to freak out.

Now—let's be honest—few people actually *want* to exercise. Nonetheless, we all desperately need to exercise. Our bodies carry around a lot of stored-up energy that needs to be released or it will turn into tension and stress. We were designed to be active, but in our modern-day world, we have the technology to be immovable blobs if we so choose. Unfortunately for those of us who find that tension and stress are triggers, we cannot afford to go without physical activity.

I have gone through seasons of my life when I have worked out a lot and seasons when I looked like I was in hyper-sleep, completely inactive. What I noticed was that working out helped me immensely with my panic disorder. Although I initially began to exercise for vanity reasons, I found I was better able to relax, sleep, and cope during difficult anxiety periods when I exercised. Consistent exercise tired me out, released stress, and increased production of helpful hormones and chemicals. As sufferers of fear, we need to exercise to give our minds a fighting chance.

The challenge in staying consistent in working out is when we don't see immediate results. For example, we might be anxious and go to the gym, but then if we don't feel a whole lot better, we believe exercise doesn't work.

I would suggest that you change your method of

measurement. Look at your symptoms and watch for change there. For example, if I don't exercise I find I'm jittery, and my legs bounce up and down when I'm seated. The result of my pent-up energy from having a desk job and a cerebral lifestyle begins to break out in subtle ways, and if I'm physically jittery, my nerves will tend to be more on edge. During a peaceful season in life, the impact of exercising is light. But during a season of heavy anxiety, exercising is crucial.

Late one December night, around one o'clock in the morning, I was in my warm, cozy bed with my wife when a panic attack began. I tried to shut it out and go to sleep, but I couldn't. I can't even remember now what I was freaking out about. All I remember is that the longer I lay there, the more I felt as though I were going insane. I finally determined enough was enough. This time I was going to do something different. I went downstairs, wrapped up like an Eskimo, and took off out the door—running.

Now, you might not believe that our area of California can get extremely cold, but I felt absolutely frozen jogging in the middle of the night. I was wrapped in a bear-sized puffy coat, complete with mittens, running through clouds of my own exhaled vapor. I was air-boxing like Rocky Balboa and muttering to myself.

My hope was that if I expended enough energy my anxiety level would drop and I would get too tired to stress out over anything. I knew exercise is a natural endorphin releaser that not only blocks out pain but also works like a sedative. And that night I needed all that.

More than anything, I wanted—I needed—a new perspective. I was wound up so tightly my cells couldn't breathe. I had to pray in a new way in a new environment. When I had tried at home in bed, my screaming thoughts drowned out any hope or help I sought. As I ran, I quickly scanned for any memories that would bring me peace or any shortcuts I could use to calm down. Then I remembered this truth: what I was currently experiencing was *not* the reality in which I lived. How I was feeling at that moment was way out of whack with who God says I am and my actual surroundings. So I sought to fix my thought process.

With each step and every labored breath, I started repeating out loud all the things that were true about me, despite what I felt. I repeated over and over, *"I'm a child of God. I'm a child of God. I'm a child of God."* Every ten minutes or so, I would change it up and start repeating another phrase, like, *"God has not given me a spirit of fear. God has not given me a spirit of fear. God has not given me a spirit of fear"* (see 2 Tim 1:7). Determined to win, I kept running and punching my fists into the air.

Eventually, the run worked. The different thinking worked. The "God phrases" worked. My new plan worked.

I went home a different man than I was when I left. God's truths slowly permeated into my brain as the exercise loosened up the receptors. I began to breathe normally. The tightness in my mind and my chest went away. My thoughts returned to a moderate semblance of peace. Thank God, at least this time, exercise made the difference.

GET ENOUGH SLEEP AND REST

Our bodies are not only set up to exert energy; they are also designed to rest. In fact, most systems in our bodies, whether our heart rates or the activity patterns of our muscles, are based on a "stress and rest" concept. Think of the traditional blipping heart signal on an electrocardiogram. The peaks are the stress points and the valleys are the rest points. Both are natural and healthy. To have only one or the other would produce a flatline, and I've heard that is very bad.

We must counteract our physical stress with appropriate rest—especially sleep. Most of us don't think too much about our sleep patterns unless we are wrestling with insomnia or disrupted sleep. Some of us actually believe we can operate on very little rest, and we scoff at the traditional eight-hour recommendation as if it's only for wimps. The truth is that we can survive on less sleep, but that doesn't mean we are functioning at an optimum level.

If I don't get enough sleep when I am dealing with stress, anxiety, or fear, I am more easily agitated and my nerves are less relaxed. I don't have as much emotional margin, and I tend to have a shorter fuse. It is interesting that an effective torture technique for interrogation is disrupting sleep patterns.

Similarly, if we are lying around too much and resting beyond what our body needs—think being a couch potato—we end up with the opposite effect; the benefit of rest is spoiled by our new need for activity. The bottom line is that our bodies need a certain amount of sleep and a certain amount of activity. To starve our bodies of sleep is to ask for more problems emotionally down the road.

But downtime isn't just restricted to sleeping at night. Our bodies and minds need rest, relaxation, and vacation time built into our schedules.

The Sabbath—a seventh day to do no work and rest—is an

original concept ordained and commanded by God. There is much value in this often discarded aspect of our modern faith.

Another great recommendation is to take two weeks of vacation all at once, if it's possible. Most people who do this report that the first week helps them unplug and relax, so they actually enjoy the second week. For our church staff, we implemented a mandatory, eight-week sabbatical every seven years to avoid burnout. If we continue to skip vacations for the sake of getting things done, we might well arrive at a place where we aren't getting anything done: a hospital bed.

How we manage our time and orchestrate our schedules will mean the difference between longevity and short-term burnout. Instead of lamenting what we cannot do, let's shift our mind-sets to deciphering what we *must* do so we can do what we *want* to do.

I want to lead my church for the long haul. I want to finish well. I want to fulfill my calling that the Lord has laid on my heart—to bring His love to tens of thousands, pray for the hurting, demonstrate Jesus to a lost world, write books, speak at conferences, grow the national ministry, and enjoy the ride. But if I'm going to do these things, certain other things need to happen. I cannot run at my natural pace and hope it's going to all fall together. I have to plan. I need to say no to some things today so I can say yes tomorrow. While a lot of those things are good—even great—I cannot do everything. I must pick and choose where I spend my energy, how I manage my body, and what I must turn down.

Although other pastors might work six or seven days a week, I can only work five or six. Even though I'm very aware that my presence at a church event leads to better attendance and helps to validate the leadership of the person running it, I can't go to most of them. I must adhere to a schedule that has me at home in the evenings, with very few late nights, so I can have downtime, healthy time with my family, and good sleep patterns. Even though it's hard to lead effectively when I'm not present, I still need to follow the sabbatical pattern, even when things aren't going smoothly in the church.

If you've ever seen me preach, it looks as though I have enough energy for days. I'm passionate, fiery, and highly demonstrative. If you didn't know better, you would swear I am Italian when I'm in the pulpit because I "talk" with my hands. What most people at our Saturday services don't know is that I take a nap every Saturday afternoon as part of my routine. I know I need to be rested and full of life to avoid stress triggers, so I schedule the nap for every Saturday and use it as a separation point between my partial day off and my workday. When I'm wise, I also go to bed at a reasonable time on Saturday nights, so that I'm refreshed for our early Sunday services (although with the nap and the adrenaline from preaching, it can be a little hard to settle down and relax).

EAT WELL

We all know a proper diet is crucial, regardless of how seriously we take the idea. I don't mean a diet to lose weight—although weight can be a significant factor in stress upon the body. Instead I mean diet as merely examining, regulating, and controlling what you eat. Certain things we ingest wreak havoc on our nervous systems and can trigger panic.

The most obvious of these substances are stimulants, especially caffeine. I have many friends who swear caffeine doesn't affect them, yet they can't even hold their hands still! What they mean is that they don't "feel different." Who said you need to feel it to know it is affecting you? Because it can trigger my anxiety, I don't drink caffeine very often and certainly not after two o'clock in the afternoon. And because I don't drink it very much, I am highly sensitive to it, which causes problems with my sleep when I do consume it. In large doses, caffeine sets my nerves on edge, especially during difficult seasons.

Another suspect is sugar. Although I don't consume very much caffeine, I do consume a lot of sugar, and it has a similar effect on me as caffeine does. It can affect my sleep and make me jumpy. When I'm wired off a stimulant, it's a bad situation in my body, especially when I'm already anxious.

As a pastor, I have to be on my game Sunday mornings so I can speak in front of thousands of people. So I get a decaf skinny vanilla latte and a parfait yogurt from Starbucks. (Such a manly morning combo, I know.) Because I'm going to infuse my body with a load of sugar through the latte, I have to eat something substantial before I arrive that morning. Usually that means something either with protein, like eggs, or a low-sugar carb of some sort. I know the flood of sugar will get my heart going and will pump energy into my body. I burn up every bit of it, though, in the energy I put forth each week in my preaching.

My main focus is guarding the hour or so before I walk out to speak. Many times I have not managed that crucial time frame well by eating inappropriately or exhausting myself in tense meetings, and I've been left fighting an unnecessary battle. The yogurt is for between the services to keep up my energy level and have something in my stomach. One of my strongest triggers is when my body gets weak and I feel light-headed. It's hard not to feel foolish for looking like a delicate flower of a man when I talk about yogurt, lattes, and the aforementioned naps. But thankfully I'm secure enough in my manhood to make good decisions, despite the occasional PR backlash. Being as diet-conscious as possible lowers my actual physical risks, thus potentially decreasing my fears.

I've noticed that managing my nutrients and vitamins can make the difference between having a panic episode and avoiding one. A doctor in my congregation provided me with a series of multivitamins, multiminerals, and phytonutrients as well as calcium-magnesium-D, omega-3, and natural B-complex supplements. I now take them daily. What I have noticed is that, whether or not they directly impact my anxiety, they make my body healthier, which in turn reduces possible triggers when I'm missing crucial nutrients.

GET REGULAR CHECKUPS

I'm not trying to sound like your mom, but I recommend physical checkups outside of care for any stress or fear disorders. Our doctors can see things that we miss. Physicians are trained to know what the human body should be doing, so they can see improper patterns and results. Let's allow them to do what they do best and get checked out regularly.

If you, like me, wrestle with hypochondria (everything to me is cancer in some form or another), doctor visits might produce a bit of anxiety. But it pays off in the end when you know what you are dealing with and gain peace of mind because a professional has taken a proper look at you. This should keep you from being alone at home at two in the morning on the Internet searching WebMD, diagnosing yourself—and freaking out.

PURSUE HOBBIES

Hobbies can offer a relaxing, restful, enjoyable, and fulfilling distraction and diversion from stress. Sometimes the fear in our lives makes us too serious, and we spend most of our time just trying to survive. But when we have seasons of respite from our anxiety, developing hobbies is a healthy way to take our minds off the intensity of life and focus on something far less important, to allow necessary downtime for restoration.

I'm into "nerd hobbies."

Collecting. I collect comic books, sports cards, rare vinyl albums, stamps, and action figures. The whole process of sorting, cataloging, and organizing is calming and soothing. When the organizational elements are done, I have a sense of closure and completion, something I rarely get as a pastor working with messy lives and dealing with matters in the eternal realm.

Jigsaw puzzles. I will sometimes break out a 1,000-piece puzzle as a challenge that will demand my full attention.

Golf. Occasionally I'll go golfing with my buddies so I can take a walk in the open air, lose some golf balls, spend money, and get really frustrated.

Marksmanship. Sometimes I go to the shooting range for target practice with my handguns. I love competing against myself and perfecting a craft. The sensory overload takes me out of my normal mind-set. I also love the smell of gunpowder, the recoil in my hands, the explosive sound, and the visual demands of the sport.

I encourage you to take time to invest in hobbies that, though they might not matter for eternity, help you relax and mellow here on earth.

We need breaks, low-stress distractions, and quiet time to stay productive in our lives. We need scheduled mental downtime when we don't have to be "on" and we can relax, allowing our minds to reorder and replenish. A healthy, organized mind can do ten times what a busy, chaotic, disorganized mind can do.

SPEND TIME OUTDOORS

I'll be honest—I'm pale enough to earn a starring role in a vampire film, so I could stand to take my own advice. Getting outdoors and into the sunlight helps us connect to healthy natural patterns and rhythms that God built into nature. Because I know you get it, rather than expand on this concept I'll just say, *Go outside!*

MANAGE YOUR CAREER

Can I go to work today?

That's a question I never want to utter, yet in my condition

I have to ask it quite a bit. I *want* to go to work—of course I do. Being a pastor is my heart, my love, and my passion. It's not a matter of whether I think I'm qualified or good at it; I believe God built me for this very endeavor. It's a question of whether I *can*. Will my body sustain me today? Will I be able to think clearly? Will I get torpedoed when I'm least expecting it?

It's not as though I can hide, right? I'm a public person. Much of my job is onstage in front of people. If I don't show up one Saturday night or Sunday morning, people are going to know. (I can just imagine it: "And now, here's Pastor Lance!" followed by the sound of crickets chirping.) It's not as though I can start meeting with a group of leaders, teaching a group of students, or preaching to a congregation and then subtly exit halfway through if I realize I can't make it the rest of the way. Yet that's exactly the scenario I find myself in more times than not.

Through the years, I have compensated for anxiety at my job in all sorts of ways. I have sat down on a stool to preach in the middle of a sermon, because I knew that at any moment I could pass out and fall over. I have had my backup guys sit in the front row, with notes in hand, waiting for the signal that they would need to fill in at that very moment. I have had the worship team prepare an extra set in case I needed more time before walking out to preach.

Praise the Lord I have never had to actually leave the pulpit for a panic attack. I have preached when I could barely see through the dizzying effects of a scrambled and anxious mind. I taught a class in the middle of my forty-day bout with attacks. More times than I can remember, I have begun preaching with no idea if I could make it past the first five minutes. One of the most frustrating aspects of my life is sitting at home, trying to recover from an episode, knowing I could be working and productive. This grates against my driven personality.

I am sure you have had to navigate similar circumstances in your own work—or whatever responsibility you have in your life that requires your optimum performance. That said, sometimes it's worth it to consider a job change. When I was first placed on medication at age twenty-four, I did a thorough inventory of my life and examined every aspect to see what healthy changes I could make. I found that I had undue and unnecessary stress in my insurance job and began to plan a way out and a transition into a new career as a pastor. Granted, pastoring eventually brought just as much—or more—stress. But instead of unhealthy stress, I deal with stress that can be managed with healthy boundaries.

I am still a work in progress and still wonder where the Lord will take me down the road. But for now, I feel very confident that I'm where the Lord wants me and I'm doing what He built me to do. Although it's hard and full of triggers, my job leaves my heart at peace and my soul full.

Can you say that? If not, can you make adjustments that would allow you to? I know this is a big step and could be scary for you, but it's worth asking the question. What is your peace and health worth to you? And what if you really enjoyed and had a passion for your new career?

—

Managing fear from the outside in is about not only doing or ingesting certain things to directly alter anxiety patterns but also living healthfully so there's less to worry about. We cannot live maxed-out all the time; our bodies won't support us. The changes I've suggested in this chapter are healthy for anyone, not just for those of us who grapple with anxiety and fear.

I'm thankful the Lord has forced healthy boundaries into my life. I hope these ideas will change your life as they've changed mine.

PART 3

LIVING IN FEAR: THE JOURNEY WITH OUR FATHER

The true children of God are those who
let God's Spirit lead them. The Spirit we
received does not make us slaves again
to fear; it makes us children of God.
With that Spirit we cry out, "Father."
—Romans 8:14–15 NCV

In part 1, I told you my story of growing up with fear looming in the background of my life, all the way into my marriage and ministry. I told you my life story through the filter of my fear so you could get to know me as a fellow sufferer.

In part 2, I gave you a great deal of the practical information I learned firsthand over many years.

I wanted to share with you as many stories and examples as possible from someone who wants desperately to offer you help, healing, and hope.

Now, here in part 3, I'm going to focus on my worldview, as shaped by *who I am* as a Christian and *what I do* as a pastor. Obviously, my faith is the driving force behind my career, and my career is a lifelong outpouring of my faith. The two are daily and forever intertwined. But both my faith as a Christian and my career as a pastor are profoundly impacted by my battle with fear. I've spent many years of my life ministering to people, and now I truly want to minister to **you** in these pages. I've talked about the physical and mental aspects of fear; now I will focus on the spiritual. Fear, anxiety, depression, and all their related issues have spiritual components.

Regardless of your background or faith journey, I pray you will open your mind and your heart for God's Spirit to reach into your soul and touch you in these chapters, as only He can.

CHAPTER 9

AS IT IS IN HEAVEN

Our anxiety does not empty tomorrow of its
sorrows, but only empties today of its strengths.
—Unknown[1]

In this chapter, we're going to look at several "big picture" elements of how Christianity intersects and interacts with fear. Your particular spiritual paradigm might include much more than I will address, or I might touch on areas in which your beliefs are different than mine. Regardless, my goal as your temporary pastor through the course of this book is to challenge you to expand your worldview, allow for your faith to grow, and deepen what you believe about God, Scripture, and your fear.

KNOW GOD IS REAL

From my many experiences, I believe some of our anxiety and fear comes from an improper view of reality. I'm not saying our threats—real or perceived—might not be legitimate; I am saying that our *reactions* to these threats are often faulty.

Simply put, we think things we shouldn't be thinking.

Worry and fear ultimately result from a belief that God is not actually in charge or that He doesn't care about us. We don't believe He is in authority or we believe He is not active in our lives. Yet neither of those statements is true. If we truly believed that God is good and He is sovereign, then we would be able to rest in these beliefs as facts. But we don't. I'd like to believe I am above such thinking, but I struggle just like you.

Some of what is so terrifying to us links to one of our deepest fears: the fear of death. At the core of many panic attacks is the idea that we (or someone we love) will die. Why? What's wrong with dying? I'm sure it's uncomfortable, but if we believe the Bible, then it's merely a transition from glory to greater glory. For the Christian, it's a step up. Why all the fuss then? Because the unknown is scary—especially events that, once done, cannot be undone.

I've read the Bible countless times, I've studied death ad nauseum, and I'm still not okay with the concept. I want to be like some of the folks in my congregation who have the attitude of, "Bring it on!" I desire to be a "walking dead man" like the apostle Paul, who couldn't wait to move on to be with Jesus. But I'm not.

Part of what's standing in my way is this darn anxiety disorder. When I'm thinking clearly and not under its influence, I'm at peace with my mortality. When a panic attack is in full bloom, however, I'm absolutely terrified of death. On good days, my reasoning and theology tell me my life is in God's hands and nothing can happen to me without His approval.

But when I'm in a bad season, every little thing seems up for grabs and comes into question.

Did you know the Bible calls death an enemy? Right there in 1 Corinthians 15:26—"The last enemy to be destroyed is death." Adam and Eve were told not to eat of the tree lest they "would surely die." God made them to live forever, but sin wrecked that plan, and death was the result. Paul says Satan has used the threat of death as a bullying technique for millennia.

Part of what Jesus Christ came to do was defeat death, by rising from the dead and making a way so those who follow Him—His children—might never truly die. They will physically die, but their afterlife with God is already secured. Death's only purpose then is to free us from this world so we might be placed safely in God's arms, delivered and whole.

The bottom line is this: Jesus *has* done the extraordinary and *has* defeated death. He took the sting—the permanence— out of it. We no longer have to fear the ramifications of the end of life. When that truth travels the short distance from our brains to our hearts, our peace will grow.

One of my favorite stories in the Bible is about the Hebrew boys Shadrach, Meshach, and Abednego (Dan. 3:1–18). They were commanded by a pagan king to bow down before his gold idol in honor of a false god. They refused to do so, so he ordered them thrown into a blazing hot furnace to be burned alive. Their response was brilliant. They said, and I paraphrase, "Our God can save us from this fire, but even if He doesn't, we still won't bow down to your false god." I love that perspective. Maybe it's one we can adopt in our hearts, one that says, "God can rescue us from all our dangers and fears. But even if He doesn't, we refuse to bow down before the bullying enemy of fear, because we know all that's truly important is already secured by God and that this life can't do anything to us." Wow! How powerful would it be if we lived that way?

This story is also proof that not all fears are irrational. It was not irrational for . . .

- Daniel to worry about the lions' den, because being eaten by large predators isn't awesome.
- Jonah to be freaking out inside a giant fish in the middle of the ocean, because usually that doesn't end well either.
- Jesus to be overwhelmed facing the cross in the Garden of Gethsemane, because what was in front of Him was unimaginable torment.

But those are the types of fears God tells us to set aside in light of who He is and what He can do. One of the greatest and most popular commands in the Bible is, "Do not be afraid." Every time God repeats this phrase, the person He is speaking to has every right to be afraid. The danger is legitimate, but God's presence overshadows all the facts. Faith is hanging on to the truth in the face of overwhelming emotional demands.

The fact is God is big—super big. He's bigger than our problems, fears, worries, and anxieties. He's actually more real than our chemically induced, warped views of life, our dysfunctional childhood patterns of thought, and our culturally derived, overblown views of who we are. There is nothing outside of His scope of authority. There is no problem too small that He would miss it or too big that He cannot solve it. Consider the following examples:

God was the One who spoke the universe into existence. Nothing was preexisting. He made it all—from nothing. Lack of materials and resources has never been a concern for Him.

> In the beginning God
> created the heavens
>   and the earth.
> The earth was barren,
>   with no form of life;
> it was under a roaring ocean
>   covered with darkness.
> But the Spirit of God
>   was moving over the water. (Gen. 1:1–2 CEV)

When the world fell into sin, the Almighty didn't sit back and ponder options with the angels. He merely put into place the plan of redemption that was prepared before the foundation of the world. God is always ahead of the curve. Nothing catches Him by surprise. No limitations sway Him. For those of us who fear, this is great news.

> In the beginning was the one
>   who is called the Word.
> The Word was with God
>   and was truly God.
> From the very beginning
>   the Word was with God. (John 1:1–2 CEV)

When God decided to flood the earth and start over with His one true follower, Noah, and his family, He initiated a plan in advance for Noah to build a boat and fill it with all species of animals (Gen. 6). Who else would have thought of that?

When Shadrach, Meshach, and Abednego were thrown into the fiery furnace to be burned alive, Jesus showed up in the fire to rescue them (Dan. 3). Who else would have thought of that option, much less actually done it?

When 185,000 Assyrians surrounded Jerusalem to destroy it, *one* angel wiped them out while they were sleeping (Isa. 37).

When Haman was going to slaughter the Jews, God used a beauty queen on the inside to turn the tables and free His people (Est. 5).

And how could God have possibly transported the reluctant prophet Jonah to Nineveh? Boat—storm—giant fish—barfed up on the beach (Jonah 2). Really? Yes, really.

God is not fazed by our problems. But we are. In fact, we freak out. So many of our anxieties aren't based in reality, but they *feel* real to us. What's the solution? We must work on getting our heads back into the game of reality—God's reality—the One who came up with *and* pulled off every scenario I listed above.

As I was going through one particularly bad season of life, my counselor shared a few thoughts that had an impact on me. She said, "The promise of a secure, positive final outcome allows peace in the present." The promise of a future deliverance allows us to dwell in what she called "impending safety." We are all familiar with "impending doom," but what if the very presence of God and our relationship with Him demanded that we view things in light of *impending safety*? What if knowing the *end* of the story helped us to embrace true life in the *midst* of the story? What if we really believed the truth that the Enemy is not stronger than our Comforter?

Although I tend to be an optimist by nature, my mind-set isn't rooted in wishful thinking but in facts that are truer than my emotions.

Just because I *feel* alone doesn't mean I am.

Just because I *think* things are unstable doesn't mean they are.

Just because I *seem* powerless doesn't mean I am.

I am wise enough to know that what I think I know isn't always right. C. S. Lewis once indicated that many of us think logic and reason are on one side of the equation and faith and emotions are on the other.[2] But that is not true. In reality, faith is based in logic (facts are why you have faith in the first place), and it's our emotions and passions that take us off the mark and distract us. In the same way, we can take comfort that what God says is true, whether or not we fully believe it. If God says we are ultimately safe, then we are, regardless of how we feel about it.

Whether our challenges and threats are fact or fabricated, our response must be to keep our eyes on Jesus and off the waves, exactly what Peter did when he walked on water to Jesus. We choose that perspective—the miraculous, not the mundane. The Enemy might be able to lure or tempt us to fixate on our problems, but it's our choice to refocus on our only solution: the Lord. We *must* ground ourselves with a solid view of who God is.

A lot of my battle with fear and anxiety is waged in my mind, in my thoughts. I am fighting a war that no one else even sees. Where my mind goes is where my body tends to follow. If I think anxious thoughts, then my body tenses up and restricts my breathing. If I can shift over to thinking about the freedom, victory, and rescue that God provides, I might get a shot at finding peace.

God gave us the ability to rally our thoughts back to reality. God tells us to keep our minds fixed on Him. He tells us that instead of looking at our troubles, we should stare unwaveringly at His face. And when God gives a command, it's a sure sign He has given us the ability to take action. Praise the Lord—we have a fighting chance!

> I have told you these things, so that in me you may have peace. In this world you will have trouble. But take heart! I have overcome the world. (John 16:33 NIV)

I fully realize that even if we get our minds in the right place, some of us still have chemical imbalances and other physical issues outside of our control that bring on anxiety. I know that mere "positive thinking" isn't going to cut it. But as I have said before, although we don't get to control our bodies, we do get to direct most of the content of our thoughts. We can choose to pray and to worship. We can choose not to dwell on the stuff that makes us freak out. Paul would not have commanded us to "take captive every thought to make it obedient to Christ" if it wasn't possible (2 Cor. 10:5 NIV).

It is not easy to submit our thoughts to God, nor will we always be successful at steering our minds. Yet that doesn't change the fact that God has placed help in front of us we can use. The more we rally the resources He gives, the better we can get at being proactive.

When our minds are solidly on the Lord, fear has a much harder time getting to us because it would have to go through Him first. When we are locked onto the power, protection, and provision of God, our anxiety has less to cling to. I can sometimes accomplish this shift by reading the Word of God. Conversations with my brothers and sisters in Christ give me a different perspective on the Lord *and* my life. Sitting in a worship service and soaking up His presence changes me. Talking myself back to what I know to be true is a gift from God. This advice is not just for pastors; this connection with the Lord is available to you as a child of God, "for God does not show favoritism" (Rom. 2:11 NIV).

Submitting to God and using His resources brings us back to where we need to be, at peace and focused. Remember, God is big enough to handle whatever is staring us down. He is mighty enough to fight all our battles. We cannot figure out every solution to every imagined trouble, but we can learn how to trust the reality that God is good and more powerful than any problems. This truth is more real than anything our fearful little hearts can concoct. If God is in control, if He is indeed the King, then His children are free to enjoy His kingdom.

Is this the way you view God? If not, great news—it certainly can be! One thing is for certain: a life focused on God is a fear-busting worldview.

STUDY THE BIBLE

I took on the task of making a full, line-by-line examination of the entire Bible on the issue of fear in all its forms. As a result, I extracted 760 passages (598 in the Old Testament and 162 in the New Testament). I found that although there are some helpful tools and instruction about some forms of fear, others are almost entirely absent from the text. For example, Jesus spoke quite a bit on the kind of fear that all people experience, but He was relatively silent on the issues of fear-based disorders.

Does this mean there's nothing to learn from His words? Of course not. In fact, the vast majority of all the helps, tips, tricks, and perspectives I have used throughout my entire life are derived from His words in these 760 passages. But we must examine the context in which He talks about fear and be careful in applying His truths appropriately to our situations. The words might be the same, but the underlying concepts are not.

Normally when the Bible refers to worry, anxiety, and fear, the text seems to discuss the practical concerns of life: basic needs, life and death, and so on. In the most popular passages of the Gospels dealing with this subject (Matt. 6:25–34; Luke 12:22–34), when Jesus says to not worry about what you will eat or drink or wear and not to be anxious about life, He is talking about not stressing out about basic needs or fretting about not being provided for. Jesus tells us to be at peace because He is the One taking care of us and, like the Good Shepherd He is, He will care for His sheep. He wants us to keep our eyes on His big picture and let Him work out the details of life. This is a necessary teaching and one that all of us should learn from, even if it's not specifically addressing anxiety disorders. We all, at one time or another, are tempted to worry about whether we will have enough and stress about how to get more. But Jesus' commands are even more important for those of us who suffer from fear, because worries about everyday life either are the heart of our actual concerns (chronic worriers) or contribute to the situational triggers of those with disorders (anxiety and panic sufferers).

The Old Testament is more limited yet more specific when talking about fear, usually referring to a justified fear of dying or something bad happening. People who feared the impending onslaught of an enemy kingdom's invasion *should* have been afraid, because they were all about to be slaughtered! When the Bible tells God's enemies to fear Him, this means they should be afraid of Him, because He can kill them and throw them into hell—literally.

That's why when God told Moses and the Israelites to not be afraid of the oncoming Egyptian army as they faced the Red Sea, His words created a tremendous shift of perspective from visual facts to intense faith in God to do the impossible. He was not rebuking the Israelites for freaking out; He was leading them to a new reality in which He was going to alter the course of nature. God was providing new information that changed their current worldview.

All our fears, whether or not they are diagnosable, have common dysfunctional triggers that the Bible informs us about. Let's learn and apply what we can. Maybe in time the words of the Lord will lead our fears to diminish, our panic attacks to stop, and our worries to subside. One thing I know for sure is that God is *really* good at healing the soul.

Jesus said we do not need to be concerned about our needs for today, nor our future. He invites us to trust Him. Jesus explained that He is paying attention; He knows our needs and is anticipating them. Although He doesn't promise to give us everything we want or ask for, He does promise to provide for our needs and take care of us.

Take time for a personal study in God's Word. What He says about fear will be beneficial to you. Here are a few references to get you started:

- God gives us perfect peace (Isa. 26:3–4).
- Don't worry about your life (Matt. 6:25–34; Luke 12:22–34).
- Don't fear man; you are valuable to God (Matt. 10:25–33; Luke 12:4–7).
- God will protect you and bring you safely home (John 14:1–4, 27–28).
- Don't let the demands of this life distract you (1 Cor. 7:32–35).
- Don't fear; instead, pray about everything (Phil. 4:4–7; 1 Peter 5:6–7).
- God will never leave or forsake you (Heb. 13:5–6).

Here are some additional helpful passages:

- Deuteronomy 1:21; 11:25; 31:23
- Joshua 23
- 1 Samuel 17:32–51; 30:1–6
- 2 Samuel 10:12; 12:15–23; 22
- 1 Chronicles 28:20
- Psalms 20:6–8; 23:4; 27:1, 3, 14; 34:4; 46:1–2; 56:3–4, 11; 112:7–8
- Proverbs 3:24–26; 12:25

- Isaiah 8:11–13; 12:2
- Daniel 10:18–19

One of the terrible lies people with an anxiety disorder deal with is that we are somehow strange, and so we are all alone in our suffering. The Devil (the Greek *diabolos* means "accuser") plays off this lie and has his team jump on every opportunity to drive us into isolation with embarrassment, crushed with shame. Fear grows in the dark and shrinks in the light. We have foolish thoughts like, *If God really loved me and I was truly a Christian, I wouldn't be dealing with this,* or *Maybe I'm having all these problems because I'm demon-possessed.*

Can't we just suffer because we are humanly broken?

Why can't we understand that being human is tough? Fear is a natural part of life. It's not always evil; it's not always due to sin; it's not always bad. Sometimes it just *is.* Fear is a reaction by a human being to an unsettling atmosphere, and as I observed earlier, we are certainly affected by our environments. Fear is part of the human condition. One of the most common commands in the Bible is "fear not." Why? Because we get scared a lot!

The Bible is full of stories of good guys and good gals being afraid. Consider the following list of amazing people in the Bible wrestling with fear and weakness:

- The disciples fearing the power of the Holy Spirit at Pentecost (Acts 2)
- Paul asking for prayer to be bold because he wasn't (Eph. 6:19–20)
- Timothy needing to be bold and not timid because

"God has not given us a spirit of fear, but of power and of love and of a sound mind" (2 Tim. 1:7 NKJV)

- Paul despairing even of life (Acts 27:20; 2 Cor. 1:8)
- Elijah being scared, depressed, and hopeless in the cave after the Mount Carmel showdown (1 Kings 19)
- Most prophets being afraid (Isa. 2:6; Jer. 1:8, 10:5, 22:25; Dan. 4:5)
- Jesus sweating great drops of blood in the Garden of Gethsemane (Luke 22:39–46)
- Paul leaving Trophimus sick in Miletus and Epaphroditus almost dying (2 Tim. 4:20; Phil. 2:25–28)

Unfortunately, without someone else with whom to process our fears, the lies and unhealthy thought patterns continue. We need to bring our fears out into the open so the Lord can heal us. Bullies last only when no one stronger is brought into the battle.

This is one of the millions of reasons why God said, "It is not good for the man to be alone" (Gen. 2:18 NIV). We were built to sort things out in community. We were meant to be ministered to, and to minister to others, in fellowship. I can't overemphasize how important it is to talk and get our fear out on the table for processing. Sometimes, just acknowledging our issues and having someone else listen and comment can pull some of the power out of the fear. Transparency is the way of Jesus, so this should be our way as well.

CHAPTER 10

THY WILL BE DONE ON EARTH

The presence of fear does not mean you have no faith. Fear visits everyone. . . . But make your fear a visitor and not a resident.
—Max Lucado, author and pastor[1]

In this chapter, we move to the aspects of Christianity and our fear that we deal with on our side of heaven—the stuff of earth.

CORRECTING UNBIBLICAL IDEAS

Even as a child, I knew when I grew up I wanted to create an atmosphere of understanding in the church for people like me. That's why I believe and teach a theology of suffering *and* healing. I strongly believe in both these contrasting aspects of faith, for God gets glory when we are healed *and* He gets glory when we struggle. He is not limited by our limitations, and we should never assume that we know exactly what He is up to, because He is indeed sovereign.

Those who have a limited understanding of the nature of God or operate strictly from a religious, legalistic point of view fall back into the unhealthy pattern of believing that if Christians do everything right, everything should go well with them. Conversely, if there is anything wrong in their lives, it must be related to their shortcomings or sins. Neither of these views is from a healthy, biblical mind-set.

Consider the character of Job in the Bible. Job was essentially selected by God as a trophy piece to show off to Satan. The Almighty started the conversation by saying, "Have you considered my servant Job, that there is none like him on the earth, a blameless and upright man, who fears God and turns away from evil?" (Job 1:8). Satan replied, "Does Job fear God for no reason? Have you not put a hedge around him and his house and all that he has, on every side? You have blessed the work of his hands, and his possessions have increased in the land. But stretch out your hand and touch all that he has, and he will curse you to your face" (vv. 9–11).

As a result of their conversation, God granted Satan permission to attack Job, who was soon left destitute, sitting in ashes, covered in sores all over his body, frightened, and confused. His marriage was in shambles and he was mourning the deaths of his children.

What did he do wrong to deserve that?

Absolutely nothing. Then why did it happen?

Valid question, right?

Because God had a bigger plan in play that required Job's suffering to bring Him appropriate glory and win the heavenly challenge brought to earth. Yet Job's friends didn't understand the big picture and refused to believe that Job could suffer and still be a good guy. Over and over, they launched a barrage of theological arrows at him, citing their worldly wisdom that if only Job would repent of his wicked ways, he would be healed and restored.

They were wrong. They were *so* wrong. In fact, in the end God threatened them with judgment for their error. The only reason they were ultimately set free was because of Job's righteous intercession and request for mercy.

Why am I sharing this incredible story with you?

Those of us with anxiety disorders already have enough to worry about without being told by our Christian brothers and sisters that we are failures or that God is mad at us. Those statements are not true and not biblical. Not all suffering is because someone did something wrong. Job's story proves this clearly.

Actually, guilt and shame tend to come more from the camp of the Enemy, the one who falsely questioned Job's faith in God. Until our friends and family in the church understand that fear and our biological responses to it are not signs of spiritual failure, they will continue to view the need for medication as a stigma. It's a lie that *all* sickness is tied to direct, personal sin.

In John 9, we discover Jesus taking on this very issue. We meet a man born blind who was healed by Jesus on the Sabbath. When the disciples first saw the man and realized he was handicapped, they asked Jesus a question that revealed their faulty theology: "Rabbi, who sinned, this man or his parents, that he was born blind?" (v. 2).

Thankfully, we have a record of Jesus' response that set them straight: "It was not that this man sinned, or his parents, but that the works of God might be displayed in him" (v. 3).

Passages like that one open up the conversation that not all sickness or trouble is due to sin and negate the idea that all Christians should be happy and healthy. How does this ideology and theology keep sticking around in light of God's truth?

Here are some more examples of biblically recorded sickness *not* tied to sin:

- Elisha's death from sickness (2 Kings 13:14, 20)
- Daniel's sickness from a vision (Dan. 8:27)
- Hezekiah's illness (Isa. 38:1–3)
- Peter's mother-in-law with a fever (Matt. 8:14–15)
- The good island chief (Acts 28:8–9)
- The faithful centurion's servant (Luke 7:2)
- The bleeding woman who touched Jesus (Mark 5:25–29)
- Jairus's daughter (Mark 5:22–23)

I am certainly not saying that sickness or suffering is *never* tied to sin. The Bible has examples of that as well:

- The death of David's child (2 Sam. 12:15)
- A good boy dies in a bad family (1 Kings 14:5–6, 10, 12–13)
- God's judgment for a broken covenant (Ex. 23:25; Deut. 7:12–15, 28:58–68)

- God's judgment on wicked King Jehoram (2 Chron. 21:15–19)
- God's judgment revealed through Jeremiah (Jer. 16:1–4)

I understand very well that there are times when God uses sickness, disease, and trouble as judgment for sin and as learning tools through consequences of bad choices. God also speaks to us through our suffering regarding changes we need to make. He uses suffering to get our attention to change. But the truth is that not *all* suffering is tied to sin. We cannot assume people who are hurting have done something wrong or their need for help indicates weakness or spiritual failure.

On the other side of the pendulum, another unbiblical idea that permeates some streams of religion is that suffering is always better than health or that it's somehow more spiritual to suffer. Do we get more "spiritual points" from God for being miserable? I'm not talking about fasting and using spiritual disciplines. I'm talking about whether you will be given more reward or praise from God if you drink a lot less water than your body really needs. How about for not going to the doctor for your broken arm? Or never taking aspirin for a headache? Choosing to walk twenty miles to work rather than drive is not more spiritual just because it's harder. Does misery somehow provide us spiritual benefit? We sometimes act as though it does. Some people have been quick to tell us it does.

But isn't there more benefit or praise from the Lord for being a good steward of what we have? And what is a good steward, after all, but one who maximizes everything he or she has by all appropriate means?

PREPARING AND WAITING

I am a realist. I would love to tell you I have a magic answer to every challenge you face, but I cannot say that. To throw pat answers at our situation belittles those of us who suffer. But one bit of wisdom I do have is to prepare during the good times. We must make healthy changes on our "up days" so we are equipped for the "down days." This requires forethought and intentional training when we are healthy.

The best time to shape our lives is when we are thinking clearly. This is the same concept young David used as he honed his skills with a sling and some rocks while watching sheep in the desert day after day, bored out of his mind. Because he practiced during his downtime, he was ready when a bear or a lion came and tried to steal one of his sheep (1 Sam. 17:34–37). Finally, with constant repetition and preparation combined with the infusion of courage from the Holy Spirit, David ran confidently into battle against the giant Goliath, certain in his ability to sling a stone into the Philistine's forehead.

Preparation is a key tool all successful people use if they want to stay at the top of their game, no matter in what industry they work. Despite his freakish natural ability, Michael Jordan was as great as he was because of his intense work ethic and drive to better himself through practice away from game time. Apart from his genetic brilliance, Bill Gates still had to do his homework in school and spend countless hours honing his gift of developing software through years of obscurity. Very few people remember that the Beatles wrote hundreds and hundreds of songs that never got recorded while they looked for the few that became number one hits. Years of practice and constant training allowed them to be ready when the spotlight hit their stage.

Developing coping skills, making healthy decisions, and learning how to manage our fear has to be a major focus for us. We must shift perspective from helpless to hopeful and learn strategies that can carry us through in times of need.

But as much as I want to proclaim hope, I must be honest. There are times when we do everything right and nothing helps. There are times when we hit rock bottom and the fear takes over. There are times when the darkness comes.

What do we do then?

We wait. We wait on the Lord.

Very few concepts irk the modern human spirit more than the demand for patience. Never before in history have people been so catered to. We don't wait for anything. But God is not on our timetable. He doesn't run at the speed of America. He has His own ways, purposes, and plans, and those plans often involve waiting.

Too often we view waiting as failing. We rely on some type of internal clock to determine whether we feel a time frame is satisfactory. Perhaps you pray for someone to be healed, and he or she isn't immediately better—but a month later you learn the person is fine and healthy. Would you deem those prayers failures because they didn't fit your timetable? Bodies only heal by the power God gives them and the systems He designs in our DNA to knit us back together. Make no mistake—any healing is God's work.

If God is sovereign, no powers can stop Him. If He is loving, there should be no qualms about rescue. If God is concerned, He doesn't need to be notified of the need. Then why must we wait? It doesn't make sense from our vantage point. But that's exactly the point—God isn't working from our vantage point or on our timetable.

God sets up systems with purposeful delay. How does a human grow? Slowly. How does nature renew? Slowly. How are some prayers answered? Slowly. Why? Because life is a process, not an event.

In Daniel 10, we are told Daniel was distraught over the state of his nation's sin and the weight of coming judgment upon Israel, and he prayed. He prayed earnestly. He prayed for weeks. Nothing happened—at least not at first.

Then an angel came to him and told him the most fascinating thing:

> Fear not, Daniel, for from the first day that you set your heart to understand and humbled yourself before your God, your words have been heard, and I have come because of your words. The prince of the kingdom of Persia withstood me twenty-one days, but Michael, one of the chief princes, came to help me, for I was left there with the kings of Persia, and came to make you understand what is to happen to your people in the latter days. (vv. 12–14)

I don't even pretend to fully understand how heavenly warfare is organized, but I can clearly see there was a moment when Daniel prayed and then there was a delay—a twenty-one-day delay, a three-week delay—before the help came.

I don't know why Daniel had to wait for his rescue. God could have given the angel more power to break through the enemy lines (as in his prior situation in Daniel 9:20–23).

God could have sent another angel to bring the message. I can think of at least ten different scenarios where God could have allowed Daniel instant help in response to his prayers, but He didn't use any of those. He made Daniel wait while the battle raged on. This account certainly helps us consider that unseen factors might be in play when we, too, must wait.

For whatever reason, God sees value in making us wait. The hope of the New Testament is contingent upon waiting for deliverance at the return of the Lord Jesus Christ, the day and hour unknown to everyone. Waiting is often how God works.

For other examples of God's people having to wait, consider the following passages:

- Exodus 24:12
- Numbers 9:8
- 1 Samuel 10:8
- Psalm 23:3
- Psalm 27:14
- Psalm 37:7
- Psalm 40:1
- Psalm 62:1
- Isaiah 40:31
- Isaiah 49:23
- Isaiah 64:4
- Hosea 12:6
- Micah 7:7
- Acts 1:4-5
- Romans 8:23-25
- Titus 2:13
- Hebrews 6:15
- Hebrews 9:28
- James 5:7-8
- 2 Peter 3:14

But what if our need is really important?

Why would God make us wait if we are in distress?

Why would He not respond immediately to the cries of His children in danger?

King Saul wrestled with the same question in 1 Samuel

13. Israel was under attack from the Philistines, and the odds didn't look favorable. If God didn't show up, the battle was going to be a bloodbath. Samuel, the national prophet and God's spokesman, told King Saul to wait seven days before engaging in warfare, until Samuel could come and offer a sacrifice to the Lord on behalf of the nation. Seven days came and went. The people started to panic and leave. Saul knew if he didn't do something quick, he wouldn't have an army left, and the Israelites would be wiped out.

Saul ordered that the altar be set up and the sacrifice prepared. He was going to offer it himself, which was absolutely forbidden. But hey, Samuel was late, right? And God was taking too long. Enough was enough. Just as Saul was coming down from the altar, Samuel arrived and asked what was going on. Saul blamed him for being late. Samuel told Saul in no uncertain terms that this was a test—and he had failed it. If he had waited as God required, he would have been secured as Israel's king. But because Saul refused to wait and allowed fear and impatience to drive his decision, God rejected him as king, and he would be replaced.

Tough lesson.

I confess. I don't like to wait. Waiting makes me anxious. Waiting makes me believe something even worse is going on. Nevertheless, God makes me wait.

In the darkest season of my life, during my forty-day battle with panic attacks, God brought no instant relief. I felt that I was left hanging, as though I had been abandoned. It seemed that God answered my prayers with a resounding no. But did He really? Who was the one who diminished my fear over time? Who sat by my side as I cried? Who took my cerebral lashes of doubt and anger, while also soothing my nerves too slowly for me to notice? Who refused to listen to *my* solutions because He had better ones of His own—in *His* time?

Exactly. My King Jesus.

HEALING

As I said before, I believe and teach a theology of suffering *and* healing. We serve a living and active supernatural God. When He says our suffering is over—it's over. When He says we are healed—we're healed. Whether or not you believe spiritual gifts, signs, and wonders are for today, we can all agree that God does the impossible and that prayer matters. You or I could be healed at any moment.

The same Jesus who touched and cleansed the leper is the Jesus whom we serve.

The same Jesus who made the blind to see and the lame to walk is the same Jesus who watches over us.

The same Jesus who fed thousands on a few loaves and fish and walked on water is our Shepherd, caring for our needs.

I know some days in this life are discouraging and hope-less, but do not lose hope. Don't let the conditions of today shape your soul forever. You might be sitting in a trial right now, but that doesn't have to consume or define you. God is not limited by our limitations and is not afraid of impossible situations. Pray as though you might be healed today. Live so that God is glorified through your suffering.

Lift your head, my friend. Salvation is on its way.

I met one of my best friends in the whole wide world in 2006. I knew her as Cushion Lady, because she would lie down in the back of the church on the floor; sitting in a chair was too painful. She lived in chronic torment from pudendal nerve entrapment—a condition where the pelvic region has the sensation of stabbing pain because the nerves are continually firing due to pressure damage. She had thirteen surgeries in fourteen years. She had everything possible removed from her lower torso in order to find a cause and cure. Her body was wrecked.

She never complained, but the agony registered on her face when she thought no one was looking. After recognizing she was extraordinarily gifted and super smart, I asked her to be my personal assistant at the church. She had to consider whether she could sit at a desk, but eventually she said yes, feeling the Lord was opening a door for her to ministry. In 2010 she came on board, and I saw one of my heroes almost every day serve people in the Lord so graciously, while hurting tremendously.

She was a praying woman. Talking to God was a whole other reality for her. Because of the excruciating pain, it took her at least two hours to get ready to leave her house in the morning. She had to pray for at least an hour and then stretch her body slowly, until she could even function as slightly normal. In her living hell she developed a depth of intimacy with God and a prayer life that I have yet to see equaled among other people. She brought that passion for prayer into my office, and I got hooked.

For almost three years, I watched her take enough meds to down a buffalo, leave work early when the pain worsened, carry a cushion to every location, tear up when the pain became unbearable, and yet never lose her faith or hope. She got prayed for more times than she could count, and by some of the most powerful prayer warriors the West Coast has to offer. But there she lay, unchanged.

She and I had a common perspective about our chronic conditions—*God will heal us when He wants to heal us, but until that day, we just keep on living with hope.* Don't get me wrong—she struggled with cynicism and doubt about healing just as much as I did, but she pressed on and continued to seek God's face.

In August 2013, she told me she was going to fly to the East Coast for a healing conference. We had been intensely studying the spiritual gifts and the power of God, so I thought nothing of the comment in the context of research, but I was stunned at the thought of her riding in a plane for so many hours.

"Are you sure?" I asked with that grandma-like face we get when we think we should be gingerly managing someone else's decisions.

"All I know is that I feel as though God is telling me to go," she flatly replied.

And she went. She went out of obedience to the Lord and a desire to know more about how He works. She didn't go with unrealistic expectations, nor was there any reason to think God would touch her there.

But He did.

On the last day of the seven-day conference, after she had been prayed for time and time again with no change, God healed her. Radically.

And I have been working with a healed woman ever since.

I know! I couldn't believe it either.

One day she suffered; the next she was walking, leaping, and praising God. And in *no* pain.

This stuff isn't just in the Bible; it still happens today. I'm an eyewitness.

And it can happen to you too.

HEAVEN MEETS EARTH

God has made us stewards and given us lives to manage, just as he gave Adam and Eve a garden to maintain. Although sin has distorted our gardens and we are broken people, God expects us to do our best with what He has put in our charge. What's wonderful is that God doesn't leave us alone in this plan. He is intimately involved in our day-to-day lives and wants to walk with us on the journey. Additionally, there are times when He, being a great Father, gives us gifts of tremendous help and hope. When the challenge of needing to make changes appears daunting, we must remember that "He who began a good work in [us] will carry it on to completion" (Phil. 1:6 NIV), and that "We are God's handiwork, created in Christ Jesus to do good works" (Eph. 2:10 NIV). While life sometimes makes us feel as though we can never change or become healthy, the Lord has given us His Holy Spirit to help us and provide us with hope.

Just in case you've never read the end of the Bible—spoiler alert: God wins. Knowing this should be encouragement enough to keep going. The resounding message of the Bible is that all those who call upon Jesus for salvation will one day be free. I despise churchy refrigerator magnet clichés more than anyone I know, but this simple, enduring truth cannot be swept aside.

No matter what you fear, *God wins.*

No matter what you think is going to happen, *God wins.*

No matter what lie the Enemy tricked you into believing, *God wins.*

The Bible is very clear about how the story on this side of eternity will end, and the climax of the story is that *God wins.* On that final day of earth, fear, pain, sorrow, and tears will be defeated once and for all. God's children will be free to experience His life and joy forever.

No matter how much we suffer *here*, we won't suffer *there*, and *there* is going to be a lot longer than *here*. No matter how confused our struggle makes us here, there we will see Him face-to-face. No matter how much we cower to the bullies of this life, our King will return and crush their heads under His boot. (Honestly, I don't know if Jesus wears boots, but it's certainly a nice visual.) We must never lose sight of the fact that our troubles are temporary. In fact, Scripture clearly says that the temporary sufferings of this world don't compare to the coming glory God has waiting for us (2 Cor. 4:16–18).

Why should we enjoy today? Because today isn't the sum total of life.

There will come a day when our hearts are free and our spirits are light.

And believe me—that day will come.

CHAPTER 11

THE THREE LIFESAVERS

A Spiritual Discipline is an intentionally directed action, which places us in a position to receive from God the power to do what we cannot accomplish on our own.
—Richard Foster, theologian and author[1]

You might guess the three lifesavers I'll offer in my pastoral guidance are the Father, Son, and Holy Spirit, but I'm going to share a different three—not the holy Trinity, but certainly a holy trio.

More than any other tools God has given us to combat fear, these three are the most powerful:

- Scripture
- Prayer
- Worship

I, like countless other Christians, cannot fathom my life without these life-saving resources. Yet, as powerful as they are, they are so familiar—almost clichéd—that believers seem to no longer trust how effective they can be in these troubled times in which we live. If you tell Christians they need to read the Bible, too many will just nod and go back to sleep. If you mention they need a prayer life, they might wholeheartedly agree but then go back to busyness. Only worship through music as a defensive weapon might be an idea fresh enough to pique any interest.

While Christians filling church pews every weekend profess belief in these practices as basic and fundamental activities for spiritual growth, our deep crisis today is that few believers actually take the time to participate in them. We own stacks of Bibles in many versions but are biblically illiterate. We know prayer can be powerful and change lives, yet we are too busy to enter into actual conversations with God. Contemporary Christian music is now a multimillion-dollar music genre, yet rarely are we in circumstances of true wonder and awe before God. We must once again go back to basics and take a fresh look at these three disciplines in which Jesus Himself engaged.

Allow me to breathe new life into these old standbys and offer a fresh reminder of some of God's greatest gifts. Let's begin with a completely different perspective on God than we might be accustomed to.

In recent years, we have sought to make God so approachable that we have erred on the side of "our buddy Jesus." We'll have a latte with Him, we'll compliment His retro hipster beard, and we'll tell Him He's a brilliant teacher. But we don't fear Him. We don't respect His authority. And what we lose in the process is a great sense of peace. We must again view God as majestic, mighty, and holy.

Until we see God as high and lifted up, as Creator and Sustainer of life, as omnipotent and omniscient, we will continue to believe our problems are bigger than He is. Until Jesus moves in our view from the pale-skinned, blue-eyed, flannelgraph rabbi into the Lion of Judah, Lord of lords, and warrior King of the book of Revelation, we will fear our enemies. The reason Scripture, prayer, and worship no longer impress us is that we have forgotten with whom we are connecting as well as what an honor it is to have such a grand and holy connection.

Where do we go to correct our view of Him?

What fresh truth can change our minds to restore our confidence in the Almighty?

How do we return to "Holy, holy, holy is the Lord God Almighty"?

Let's dive in.

SCRIPTURE

In God's Word, we find absolute truth in an ever-shifting world of cultural relativity. By reading the Bible, we can renew our minds and recalibrate our worldviews. As I said before, for good or bad, our worldviews are so powerful that what we think, we do. Doomsday preppers believe in imminent danger, so they stockpile supplies for the day the world falls apart. Conspiracy theorists are so suspicious of the government that they will go to extreme lengths to get off the technological grid in search of anonymity. Some monks and nuns believe God is most honored by withdrawing into seclusion, so they spend their entire lives in solitude. What we believe becomes our reality.

But what happens when we recognize our worldviews are faulty?

What happens when we realize how we see things is not accurate?

What happens when we react based on those false beliefs and they hurt us?

No human's worldview is fully accurate. Each one of us has errors in how we think the world works, and when we are wrong, bad things tend to happen. For those of us who are susceptible to worry, fear, and anxiety, something within our worldview sees reality as inherently unsafe—whether or not it is. The only way to combat such a view is to be convinced otherwise.

The Bible shows us God's worldview. Within its pages, He reveals His world and how we should see it. When we read and understand Scripture properly, our worldview shifts to one more accurately aligned with God's reality: He is almighty and sovereign in His control. When we are linked with God through what Jesus did on the cross, we are given the right to become His sons and daughters, adopted into the family of God with a new identity. This transformation shifts our standing in this world, and this new perspective on the world becomes true for us.

Humans are leaky vessels. What we once knew, we have soon forgotten. What was once certain is now fuzzy and obscure. Distractions, time, and personal passions erode our Christian faith and understanding of what is right and true. In the modern world, the number of distractions has increased exponentially, because we now have all manner of media. We are bombarded with new ideas, challenges, and distorted truths nearly every moment of every day.

A return to the truth of the Bible resets and refocuses our minds and hearts on what is good, right, holy, and healthy. We need to be reminded that God is in control and Satan is contained. We need to be reminded that our God is not limited by our physical laws. Our problems—no matter how big they are—do not scare our Lord. Just as Peter was able to walk on water when he looked into the eyes of Jesus and sank when he looked away, so too are we transported from our troubles into the loving arms of a secure God when we look to His *Word* and take His *words* to heart.

We have so many distorted views to dispel. When we read the Bible, we learn we are not to fear what other people think of us or can do to us. When we read the Bible, we think twice about our rat-race mentality and begin to take up what Christ referred to as His easy yoke and light burden (Matt. 11:28–30). The key to reading the Bible as the text was intended is taking the time to allow the words to soak into our hearts and minds so we don't just *hear* the words but also *own* them. Sometimes this means we need to memorize verses and passages that speak specifically to our condition. These are some of my favorite verses I meditate on:

- "Have I not commanded you? Be strong and courageous. Do not be afraid; do not be discouraged, for the LORD your God will be with you wherever you go" (Josh. 1:9 NIV).
- "The LORD is with me; I will not be afraid. What can mere mortals do to me?" (Ps. 118:6 NIV).

- "For God has not given us a spirit of fear and timidity, but of power, love, and self-discipline" (2 Tim. 1:7 NLT).
- "The LORD is my light and my salvation—whom shall I fear? The LORD is the stronghold of my life—of whom shall I be afraid?" (Ps. 27:1 NIV).

One of the greatest things about reading Scripture is that the words are hope filled and hope inspiring. We read of the Deity who interjects Himself into the affairs of His creation. We see the God who does miracles. We see the God who rescues by extraordinary means at extraordinary times. When we are in the midst of a panic attack, we need a Deliverer, and we need Him *now*!

I think everyone in the world, deep down, has an innate sense that God is real and our only hope in crisis. This is why when we are in emergency situations, our first inclination is to cry out to God for help, whether or not we have a relationship with Him. We know He can help us. Whether He will intercede and rescue us is another discussion, but we certainly know He *can*. When we are overwhelmed with fear, we need to read about someone who can help us. We need to be transported from frail hopelessness to hope and expectation. Sometimes just being reminded that God is in charge and has our best interests in mind is enough to soothe some of the discomfort.

PRAYER

More than any other help, hint, or hope I will write about in this book, prayer is what I have used most often and what gives me the most blessing. The Bible says God's ears are attentive to His children. He doesn't promise to give His kids everything we want, nor does He promise He will remove all our problems. Scripture does say, however, that when we are hurting, afraid, worried, or in trouble, we can call out to Him and He will respond. Of course, we would love that response to be an ever-present yes, but then again, that would make God a divine dispensing machine or a cosmic Santa, and He is certainly not those.

God will answer the prayers of His people with one of three responses: yes, no, or not yet.

Usually our prayers go something like this: *God, I'm freaking out! Fix it!* A yes answer has a relatively immediate soothing and calming effect, whether through natural or supernatural means. A no answer is God's decision to let whatever we are concerned about happen—or not—so that something greater will occur according to His plan. A not yet or wait answer brings little to no relief initially, but a chain of events is launched and, in time, comes around to solve the problem.

But what about when we *can't* pray?

Have you ever been in such fear or despair you cannot even lift a single word toward heaven? I have. (Praise the Lord that the Holy Spirit intercedes for us when we don't have the words see Rom. 8:26.) What do you do then? You call in reinforcements.

During my forty-day panic attack, a senior pastor of another church who is a dear friend of mine contacted me. He knew I was hurting, broken, and really going through a rough time. He called and asked if he could come over to my house, which is thirty minutes from him. He doesn't like driving in unfamiliar areas, but he wanted to visit, lay hands on me, and pray over me. I said yes more out of respect for him than out of any expectation for any sort of breakthrough.

At the scheduled time, the doorbell rang, and as I opened the door, a strange man greeted me with, "Hi, Lance." I was a bit put off at first, wondering who this guy was. But then over his shoulder I saw my friend waiting to give me a hug. I then put it together that they were a dynamic duo coming to save the day. After being introduced to my friend's friend, I realized that, indeed, I had already met him, but in my rattled state I hadn't recognized him.

They listened to my story of how upside down I was. Next, they gathered around me with my wife, laid hands on me, and prayed. It was so nice to listen to trusted voices praying truth and protection over me when I lacked the strength to do it myself. Feeling lifted up by my friends, when my soul was so burdened down, was so sweet. To me, intercession is one of the greatest gifts we can give one another.

I believe in the power of prayer so much that I have an intercessory team whose members take turns praying and fasting for me to support the office I hold and the calling on my life as a minister of the gospel. I consider them my "spiritual bodyguards" and have seen direct results from their watch over me. I also believe strongly in the verse that says, "We who are strong have an obligation to bear with the failings of the weak" (Rom. 15:1). In my strong seasons and on my strong days, I pray with other people through their hurt with all my heart, knowing the power of intercession in my own life.

To encourage you about the power of prayer and to provide evidence to support my viewpoint, allow me to share with you an incredible passage from Scripture:

Therefore, confess your sins to one another and pray for one another, that you may be healed. The prayer of a righteous person has great power as it is working. Elijah was a man with a nature like ours, and he prayed fervently that it might not rain, and for three years and six months it did not rain on the earth. Then he prayed again, and heaven gave rain, and the earth bore its fruit. (James 5:16–18)

Additionally, here are a few Bible stories where the outcome hinged on God's working through the prayers of His people:

- Isaac prayed for his barren wife, Rebekah, and she had twins: Jacob and Esau (Gen. 25:21).
- The prayers of Moses stopped the judgment fire of the Lord from consuming the Israelite camp, stopped the poisonous snakes from killing many more people, and stopped God from killing Moses' brother Aaron, as well as purified his sister's leprosy (Num. 11:2, 21:7; Deut. 9:20; Num. 12:13).
- The barren Hannah prayed for a child and was graced with one of the greatest prophets ever, Samuel (1 Sam. 1:10).
- Samuel's prayer for Israel rescued them from the invading Philistines (1 Sam. 7:8–10).
- A prophet's prayer restored a king's withered hand (1 Kings 13:6).
- King Hezekiah's prayer to heal his illness was granted when God added fifteen years to his life (2 Kings 20:1–11).
- Jonah's prayers of repentance got him vomited back out of the great fish (Jonah 2).

I could go on and on, but I want to set appropriate expectations regarding prayer. Sometimes when we read stories like the ones I mention above, we can get the impression that all we have to do in a bad situation is toss up a half-hearted prayer. Then God, the "magic genie," will come to our rescue. Nothing could be further from the truth. Prayer is a serious discipline, not a "call button" for summoning God like the button a patient presses to summon help from a hospital nurse.

True prayer is supposed to be a relational communication with a God you know deeply and personally. This doesn't mean you can't pray unless you know God super well. We all have to start somewhere. I am merely saying we cannot whimsically pray, as if we are ordering from a takeout menu over the phone.

We see that Jesus faced trial after trial and consistently went to prayer for His solutions and guidance. What we tend to forget are passages like Luke 6:12, which says, "In these days he went out to the mountain to pray, and all night he continued in prayer to God." He prayed all night! If prayer were easy and quick, why did He do that? This was the night before He selected the twelve men to whom He would hand over the ministry when He returned to heaven—a decision that required a serious conversation with God.

And we forget the Garden of Gethsemane, where Jesus seemed to hear no response at all. Why else would He pray the same request, verbatim, three consecutive times? But in the end, He got a no answer; God did not deliver him from his suffering. My point is simply this: prayer matters, but it is not a manipulation tool, nor is it to be treated lightly. Our God wants to minister to us, but we must trust that He knows what He's doing and He knows better than us.

Sometimes we are going to pray and God will come through with a miracle. Other times we are going to pray with all our hearts and our situation will seem to remain unchanged. Nevertheless, prayer was designed for connection and transformation, even more than for altering the circumstances of our lives. If we pray to the One we know and love and still hear a no, we must lean back into faith and trust that God is good and in control. He has a plan in play that we couldn't comprehend even if we tried.

WORSHIP

The third component of my holy trio is worship. By definition, worship is anything that attributes worth to someone or something. Singing songs of worship is only one form of exaltation, but it's still a powerful tool in the life of a believer and the specific form I want to discuss here.

Let me say up front that this is the area in which I have the least ministry expertise. I am flying blind on this one to some degree. Although I spent the majority of my younger days in a Christian band and thought I would be a musician for my career, I still don't know how to connect in worship through music very well. But personal experience and biblical evidence have given me respect for worship as a tool for spiritual warfare.

When I was in my early teens, something happened that I will never forget. It was late at night, around midnight, and I was tucked into my bed, surrounded by my '80s black lacquer bedroom set and my walls covered in Stryper posters. Only my mother and I were in the house.

To this day, I don't know if what I saw was a dream or a vision. But as I lay there, I was overcome by a tremendous sense of evil. Suddenly, what seemed to be a pile of wood with glowing green embers inside appeared over my bed. Unable to escape from the abject terror of the sensation of darkness, I couldn't think clearly enough to realize that a pile of wood is a silly thing to be afraid of. I was too caught up in the gripping panic. Immediately, I prayed for this image to go away, but it didn't. I shut my eyes in hopes I was merely dreaming, but when I opened them, it was still there. I knew if I sat up I would be within inches of the object, so after a few moments of trying to pray it away to no avail, I slipped down to the side of my bed, keeping my distance from the thing.

I knelt at my bedside with my eyes closed, knowing the more I looked at it, the more afraid I became. I prayed harder, but it wouldn't budge. Convinced that I was going to fall apart under the fear, I scrambled to think of anything else that would help. Then I thought of worshiping. Right there, kneeling at my bedside, I began to quietly sing all the praise songs I knew. After the second song, the fear began to subside. After a few more songs, I felt the presence had left, and with a quick glance up, I confirmed my suspicion.

Prayer alone didn't dismiss whatever it was, but adding worship did. The Bible says there is power for spiritual warfare in worship, and I saw this firsthand.

For whatever reason, God uses music to create an atmosphere for His engagement. Consider the situation of the first king of Israel, Saul. You won't find a more complex Bible character. At one point in his career, God pulled His blessing and anointing from this man and sent in their place an evil spirit to torment him (1 Sam. 16:14–23). When Saul's servants saw this happen, they suggested he hire a young man to play a musical instrument called a lyre so he would be soothed and the evil spirit would leave. How did they know that would work? I'm not sure, but it did. Right there in verse 23 is the evidence: "And whenever the harmful spirit from God was upon Saul, David took the lyre and played it with his hand. So Saul was refreshed and was well, and the harmful spirit departed from him." How bizarre.

Why would God want to use music and worship as a means of pushing away an evil spirit? Why didn't He use another method? I don't know. (I say that a lot, because, well, I don't.) But I do know God didn't do it only once. He used worship in song as a spiritual weapon many times. One of my favorite times is when the walls of Jericho came tumbling down (Josh. 6).

The ancient city of Jericho was, for all practical purposes, impregnable; the walls were incredibly wide and thick and designed to withstand any attack. But the walls could not stop God, who used most unusual means to help the Israelite army get past them. He commanded Joshua and the army of Israel to march around the city once a day for six days with the priests playing their trumpets. On the seventh day, they marched and played seven times and, on the final lap, they stopped. They sounded the trumpets, everyone in the army shouted for the Lord, and the walls came crashing down. Israel won the city. What a weird strategy!

Perhaps the most clear but unusual occurrence of warfare

through worship is the story of King Jehoshaphat, the king of Judah (Southern Israel). Second Chronicles 20 records how Judah was attacked by three mighty enemy nations. The king called for a national prayer and fast. God responded that He would fight for them. And then the most wonderful verse says, "And when they began to sing and praise, the LORD set an ambush against the men of Ammon, Moab, and Mount Seir, who had come against Judah, so that they were routed" (v. 22). In this case, worship turned into actual, physical warfare against a real, live enemy.

—

As a pastor with anxiety, I get the weirdest recommendations, some of which you wouldn't believe if I told you. Different seasons call for different measures, and some are a little out there. During my terrible forty-day period of anxiety, one friend said she felt the Lord encourage her to tell my wife and me to begin a period of thirty days of soaking in worship and taking Communion every day as a couple. When you are desperate, you'll try almost anything. Trust me, I know. And so we began.

At first, it was absolutely awkward. I lay on the couch, and Suzi sat in a nearby chair. We turned on a worship song. We don't normally just lie around and listen to music together, so this took some getting used to. As a driven personality, doing nothing but listening to other people worship was hard. But I think doing nothing was the point. This was about receiving, letting worship to the Lord wash over us, and letting God be glorified as He fought the battle. For this very reason, my wife plays worship music every morning as we all get ready for the day.

As suggested, we also took Communion, which was also a tad awkward. But we did it, and I'm thankful we did. We will never know the power of those thirty days, how much they blessed our souls, and how much God moved during that time. But we knew seeking God's face and resting in His praise was wise and right.

I want to clarify that worship is not a dispenser of peace on command. There are times when it is effective in a traceable and tangible manner, and there are times when it's not. Nevertheless, know this:

There is power in the Word of God.

There is power in prayer.

There is power in worship.

Why? Because they are all routes to the King of kings, the One who wields all the power. We must never think the power lies in the plan, because it lies in the Person. He has given us access to Him when we are in need, as well as an invitation to abide in Him every day.

I recall a conversation with some wise friends about what it means to abide in Christ. The conversation turned to the fruit of the Spirit, as mentioned in Galatians 5:22–23. Many of us look at the compilation there as a to-do list of virtues we need to work on: love, joy, peace, patience, kindness, goodness, faithfulness, gentleness, and self-control. But that is not all the fruit is about. When our roots are solid and healthy in Christ, we will naturally produce those "fruit" in our lives. A healthy apple tree doesn't have to struggle to make apples; it just does. In the same way, a healthy Christian doesn't have to struggle with love, because it flows naturally.

You and I struggle in the area of peace. Instead of saying we need to strain to be more peaceful, the more appropriate response is to get closer to Jesus, allowing the Holy Spirit to bring us to peace His way. I'm not saying if we were only closer to God, everything would be fine. Even Job knew that's not true. But ultimately our peace is in the hands of our Shepherd, not left to us, the frail sheep.

CHAPTER 12

BECOMING A BATTLE-READY BELIEVER

The first step on the way to victory
is to recognize the enemy.
—Corrie ten Boom, author[1]

Is our struggle with fear Satan's doing?

Is it caused by spiritual warfare?

Are demons flying around, clamping on to people and driving them into fear?

Are angels shielding us from supernatural assaults?

Is this fear the result of being human?

Is it a physical manifestation of something broken deep down?

Are our symptoms caused by a natural body reacting to natural stimuli with natural results?

My answer to all these questions is *yes*.

I do not believe the *majority* of our problems with worry, fear, anxiety, and panic are due to supernatural causes. I believe most of them can be dealt with and handled in the physical realm with the normal interactions of the body. But when events with no rhyme or reason start happening, that fit no predictable patterns, or that come completely out of left field, I tend to think something supernatural is afoot.

Let me tell you a story.

Bare naked, the man ran at Jesus and His disciples in all of his hairy, grimy glory. They could smell his stench from twenty yards out, and he showed no signs of slowing down as he barreled down upon them. Hair matted, bone-skinny with nails like an eagle's talons, he screamed as he ran. From what Christ's crew could make out, the garbled words were something about begging Jesus not to torment him.

What was this guy talking about?

As he often did in his assumed role, Peter was just about to step in front of the Lord in defense when the man dove headlong to the ground. He came skidding to a halt in a cloud of dust at the Master's feet. Sobbing and stumbling over his words, sunburned lips caked in dried spittle and with foam coming from his mouth, he couldn't seem to form any articulate words. Thankfully, there was a pig farmer nearby, who rushed over to see if everything was okay. He knew this man well (we'll call him "Josiah") and told Jesus and the disciples his story. Although his story is not recorded in Scripture, I picture it going something like this.

Josiah was once a respected member of the community. He worked hard and was an honest man. Prone to depression and a natural introvert, he kept to himself and lived with his older brother Micah. As time passed, Micah noticed Josiah was getting involved with some questionable people outside of town who were rumored to be engaging in some bizarre rituals. Then one day Josiah didn't come home.

After a few days, Micah set out in search and located Josiah in a deserted alleyway, mumbling incoherently. Just two days later, Josiah went missing again. Micah found him, but again, Josiah escaped. Eventually, Micah gave up trying to contain Josiah and let his brother go.

Months later, Micah was awakened by someone pounding on his front door. When he answered, there stood an old friend. He told Micah to come quickly. Josiah was in trouble. Micah ran with his friend to the outskirts of the village, where they could hear the sounds of a shouting mob and piercing shrieks from some unearthly, ungodly force. As they pushed their way through the crowd, Micah saw his brother cornered against a wall, snarling and raging at his attackers. Bloody slash marks covered his body.

"What have they done?" Micah cried.

"The people didn't do that. Josiah did it to himself. Those are self-inflicted wounds," the friend replied. "He's been cutting himself with rocks."

Micah held up his hands and shouted to get the attention of the men holding Josiah at bay. They quieted for a moment and let him approach his younger brother. Josiah's eyes were wild with fear. He appeared to not recognize Micah at all, nor could he seem to focus on reality. He acted like a trapped wild animal as his brother reached out his hand to comfort his tormented sibling. In a split second, Micah found himself on his back in the dirt with a stinging cut over his left eye. Josiah had rushed at him and swung the broken chains around his wrist at his brother's head. Retreating back into the corner, Josiah began to wail.

Micah understood now that Josiah's condition was too far gone for any of them to help him. He begged the crowd to back up and let the madman, who was once his beloved brother, go. Reluctant, they made an opening, and the demon-possessed body bolted for the clearing and ran off into the distance.

That had been the last time the villagers had seen Josiah. The village elders had written him off, and people pretended he didn't exist, even though everyone knew he lived among the desert tombs. If anyone dared to get within half a mile of there, they could hear him wailing and moaning, day and night. But he had stayed away from people—that is, until today. When he saw Jesus.

This is where the Bible picks up the story.

Suddenly, deep, anguished tones gushed from Josiah's mouth as he said, "What have You to do with us, Jesus, Son of the Most High God? Have You come here to torment us before the time? I beg You, I adjure You by God, do not torment us."

"What is your name?" Jesus calmly asked.

"My name is Legion, for we are many," came their replies.

Neither Peter nor any of the other disciples knew what to do. They had handled demon-possession before, but they had never heard so many voices at once and someone speak in the plural like this poor soul. "This man must have many demons," they said to each other. And, indeed, he did— hundreds, if not thousands. Only Jesus knew.

The demons began begging the Lord to send them into the nearby herd of pigs on the hillside if He was going to cast them out. They pleaded not to be forced into the abyss, where they knew they would be sealed until the Day of Judgment. Jesus granted their request and cast them out into the swine.

Josiah, now up on his knees, tilted his head back and let out a shrieking cry. All the pigs began to squeal and the herd rushed down the embankment into the water below, drowning themselves. Josiah fell facedown before Jesus, as if dead.

After a while, he got up and came over to join the band of disciples. I can only imagine that everything about him was different. His eyes, skin tone, even the way he carried himself. There was a lightness of his being, a calm and ease to his demeanor. He came to the Lord and poured out his gratitude. Jesus asked Philip to give the man a tunic and invited Josiah to sit down to eat with them. Now sharp, alert, and desperately thankful, Josiah ravenously ate the meal.

After a brief conversation with the frightened locals demanding that Jesus leave their area, Jesus' group headed down to the boat to return home. The man followed them to the water's edge, asking if he could join their team and dedicate his life to serving Rabbi Jesus. The Christ graciously told him to go home to his friends and family and tell them how much the Lord God had done for him, how He had mercy upon him. The man agreed and went back home, proclaiming to the entire village about his freedom.

Many of you will recognize this as a creative retelling of the story of Legion, written about in Matthew, Mark, and Luke. Because the demon-possessed man's story is one of my favorite accounts in the Gospels, I took the liberty of creating a backstory for him.

This testimony must have caused quite a stir to be included

in all but one of the Gospels. I love this story because the power of God to transform even the most hopeless of people is brought to life. It also gives us insights into how spiritual warfare works and what the Enemy is up to. One absolutely crucial point for our purposes is this: just as God has a plan for our lives, Satan does as well, meant only for his evil and our harm.

Countless sermons have been given about God's will for the lives of His people, and rightfully so. But have you ever considered Satan's will for your life? If he had his way, what would your life look like? Exactly what we saw with the story of Legion: full-on control. Anything Satan and his team can do to make you look more like Legion, they will—through isolation, self-harm, hopelessness, shame, fear, and on and on.

I do not believe the core catalysts for the majority of issues dealing with worry, fear, anxiety, and panic are directly demonic in origin, although they—as all infirmities—have their source in original sin, which Satan helped bring to man. I do, however, think *Satan does not hesitate to try to capitalize on the problems and make them worse.* Whether we start the train rolling or he starts it doesn't matter; he will still try to derail our lives wherever and whenever he can.

Satan's goal seems to be focused on wanting to hurt or distort what God loves. And what does God love? His creation. What does God love most in His creation? Mankind. And there you have it: anything the Devil can do to harm us, he will do.

If our selfishness begins the process of greed, the Devil will enhance the lure. If our broken nature twists our ambition into pride, the Devil will fan the flame. If someone abuses us out of dysfunction, the Devil will try to exacerbate the issue.

I'll be clear: Yes, I believe in spiritual warfare and, yes, I believe spiritual warfare can be at play with anxiety, worry, and fear. But I don't play the game of blaming *everything* on the Devil and giving him undue credit. I believe in looking at the facts and calling them as they are. As with all of life, including the spiritual, there is a balance.

The supernatural is real. God and the Devil are real. Angels and demons are real. Why then wouldn't those supernatural forces play a part in the lives of humans? Of course they do. The question is, what do we do about it when they show up?

All my life I've battled with fear based in the supernatural. For some unhealthy, bizarre, and dysfunctional reason, God gets drawn into my fears almost as much as Satan does. I have an irrational fear that God will reject me or that somehow I'll miss out on His offer of salvation. Of course, this is not true, and on my good days, I'm absolutely secure in my faith. But on the days when panic hits, it's a whole other story.

It's so ironic that the source of my greatest peace can also be used as a tremendous source of torment. The reason these issues play so strongly in my particular wrestling match with fear is that in my worldview, the supernatural world is all that truly matters. I consider the unseen more real than what I live in day to day. I've grown up with a perspective of life designed by God and shaped by Scripture. If everything in this world is ultimately going to burn and be redeemed, then shouldn't I put all my bets on the eternal? There's only one problem: the supernatural is the one place I have almost no control at all. Hence the trigger for fear.

If I believe the Bible is true, then I believe that when

the apostle Paul talks about spiritual warfare, he's talking about something more real than the Battle of Gettysburg! Unfortunately, what this means for someone like me—a person with an overactive mind who runs constant mental scenarios for safety—is that I try to account for ten times the number of dire circumstances beyond what I can see and touch. This is not good. There are too many variables and too many what-ifs, so I have to rein in my thoughts and not let them go wild. After all, Satan is a bully, and bullies prey on fear to take advantage. If they can convince us something is true, even though it isn't, they can manipulate us.

As a C. S. Lewis fan, I can't help but add my favorite quote of his in regard to the demonic, taken from his book about spiritual warfare, *The Screwtape Letters*: "There are two equal and opposite errors into which our race can fall about the devils. One is to disbelieve in their existence. The other is to believe, and to feel an excessive and unhealthy interest in them."[2] This fascinatingly creative and nonthreatening work exposes the tricks Satan uses to trip us up. In that same spirit, I want to go a bit deeper into spiritual warfare to uncover some of the Devil's traps and prepare you to fight back. What are the rules of engagement for spiritual warfare? When do they apply? How much access does Satan have to believers? How much attack does God allow? Why would He allow any at all?

All true Christians have the indwelling Holy Spirit within them, and God is not going to share real estate with Satan or demons. But I think sheer experience and biblical examination demonstrate that God will let the bad guys go pretty far in their attacks before He tells them to back off. Job's story makes that quite clear.

Satan is not an equal power against God, because he is a created being. We serve an immeasurably greater Creator who is sovereign over all. Remembering this paradigm is absolutely paramount when dealing with any form of spiritual warfare. We must do all we can to discern when warfare is at play and shut it down, while simultaneously hanging on to the fact that the Lord Jesus Christ, through His work on the cross, marked the end of an era of bullying fear that Satan had ravaged on the world up to that point. Because Jesus Christ is alive and on His throne, the war has been won. Battles are still being fought and there will still be casualties, but the end result is certain.

Satan has used the same strategies throughout history to try to destroy, or at least mar, mankind. Why change the scheme if it keeps working? His usual bag of tricks seems to have success.

Let's begin with two of his best weapons—guilt and shame. If Satan can convince us we are worthless failures, he wins in this life. He does this through condemning us for our weaknesses, failures, and sins. He is most successful when we react to an attack with self-destructive behavior. How brilliant to get one's opponent to do the work for you! He can stop beating us up, because we take over beating ourselves up.

His ultimate goal is to drive us to hopelessness—the belief that no one and nothing can help us out of our condition—so we will give up. We combat this tactic by allowing what Jesus Christ did for us on the cross to free us from any condemnation of failure. We admit that we are weak, but we do not consider our weakness to be a valuation of our worth. Being broken is okay. Being weak is entirely normal. Here we let

God fight the battle of our merit, because He has already won. Read these three versions of Romans 8:1 to let this fact sink into your spirit. God has made this point quite clear:

Therefore, there is now no condemnation for those who are in Christ Jesus. (NIV)

So now, those who are in Christ Jesus are not judged guilty. (EXB)

If you belong to Christ Jesus, you won't be punished. (CEV)

Another wily snare Satan uses to bring us down through fear is the temptation to take shortcuts. Although we could get what we crave through healthy means, we feel it would take too long, so the Enemy provides a shortcut for us to get the same result much faster and with less work. A simple example would be to go for the Twinkie instead of the lean turkey sandwich. Another would be to self-medicate through drugs and alcohol rather than follow the proper path to deal with anxiety.

The third test the Devil brought against Jesus during the forty-day temptation in the desert was offering Christ all the kingdoms of the world and their glory, if only He would bow down before him. This was a shortcut around the cross and to where Jesus was already going. Jesus would indeed get all the kingdoms of the world and their glory, but it was going to come God's way—through suffering and extreme cost. Satan was offering a faster, easier solution, but it was a trap. Jesus knew and turned him down flat.

The final tactic that relates to our dealings with fear is Satan's use of doubt. Ever since the garden of Eden, the Father of Lies has been asking questions that beg doubt in the minds of believers.

Satan said to Eve, "Did God actually say, 'You shall not eat of any tree in the garden'?" (Gen. 3:1). When Eve replied that God said they would die if they ate of that particular tree, Satan infused doubt again, contradicting the word of the Lord by saying, "You will not surely die" (v. 4), and then went on to explain to her and Adam the benefits of rejecting God's plan.

All it takes is a few pointed questions to get us thinking that maybe God isn't good. Maybe God has abandoned us. Maybe we are alone. This is why I think it's so common for people who wrestle with fear to also wrestle with an unhealthy view of God. Worrying about losing one's salvation or feeling cursed or judged by God only adds to the mental suffering. Those are all bullying tactics to get us to run away from our one sure hope and salvation.

Satan is the king of what-if scenarios. Because he lacks the power to create, he can only distort. Because he isn't able to dictate the future, he has to resort to manipulation. And he's good at it. How much time have we spent worrying about scenarios that never come to pass? Exactly. The more energy we spend worrying, the less time we spend focused on God's purposes and protection. The more distracted he can make us, the less we are advancing the Lord's kingdom.

Hide in your heart these important truths of the Bible:

- As brilliant and powerful as Satan is, God is infinitely greater. "Little children, you are from God and have overcome them, for he who is in you is greater than he who is in the world" (1 John 4:4).

- We know that God is not the one trying to terrify His children; that is the work of the Enemy. "For God gave us a spirit not of fear but of power and love and self-control" (2 Tim. 1:7).
- We know God ferociously protects His own. "My sheep hear my voice, and I know them, and they follow me. I give them eternal life, and they will never perish, and no one will snatch them out of my hand. My Father, who has given them to me, is greater than all, and no one is able to snatch them out of the Father's hand" (John 10:27–29).
- We know that as children of God, we do not have to fear wrath from our Father; therefore, accusations from the Enemy fall flat. "What then shall we say to these things? If God is for us, who can be against us? He who did not spare his own Son but gave him up for us all, how will he not also with him graciously give us all things? Who shall bring any charge against God's elect? It is God who justifies. Who is to condemn? Christ Jesus is the one who died—more than that, who was raised—who is at the right hand of God, who indeed is interceding for us" (Rom. 8:31–34).

As an added encouragement, let me share a helpful perspective on 1 Peter 5:8: "Be sober-minded; be watchful. Your adversary the devil prowls around like a roaring lion, seeking someone to devour." Some scholars believe this verse is actually referring to a desperate lion, not a victorious one.

The animal is roaring in hopes of scaring up some rodents to reveal themselves from underground for a meal. Normally lions don't roar when stalking large game, because this scares it away. But if the lion is left with no options other than starvation, he's going to try to scare up some appetizers. Whether or not this interpretation is accurate, the truth remains that when Jesus is the bodyguard, the Deliverer, Satan's hopes of destroying God's children are dashed. Nevertheless, the Devil is a tenacious being, and if he can't win he will certainly do his best to make sure no one gets to enjoy the ride.

Be encouraged, my friends. I know spiritual warfare sounds scary, and the whole idea of Satan out there lurking like a lion seems frightening. But take heart. Our God is greater and He has overcome!

Demons know who Jesus is. They know whom they are up against. They understand how the supernatural works more than we do (James 2:19). Consider for a moment how demons reacted to Jesus Christ when He was here on earth. In both the story of Legion from the Gerasenes region I told earlier and the instance of the man with the unclean spirit in the Capernaum synagogue (Luke 4:31–35), the demons all cried out in fear when they saw Jesus and begged Him not to destroy them. It's abundantly clear that the demons see Jesus for who He really is: the King of kings and Lord of lords, who rides on a white horse with blazing eyes and a sword, sweeping His enemies away.

Not only are we safe, but the terror is on the other team. The only way the Devil is going to get any true authority in our lives is if we buy into his lies and allow ourselves to be enslaved by him. He might be able to volley fiery darts into our minds, but whether we allow ourselves to believe that we are held hostage in a prisoner of war camp is on us. Slavery is built on fear and lies of the mind. The more we focus on the great ferocity of our almighty God during the calm and quiet days, through reading the Bible and prayer, the more the power of the Enemy begins to pale.

The outcome of the war over mankind is so certain that the biblical descriptions of spiritual warfare on the side of the believer are to simply stand and resist (Eph. 6:10–20). While fighting a battle by only holding our ground might sound silly, our job description is clear—to hold. And if the battle isn't in reality ours, but God's, then it only makes sense to wait while He finishes the fight.

Take a look at a few passages about battling the Devil, and perhaps you will be as surprised as I was to see how many of them show our responsibility as not offensive but defensive, and lend to the idea of holding ground rather than taking ground.

- "Your adversary the devil prowls around like a roaring lion, seeking someone to devour. *Resist him*, firm in your faith, knowing that the same kinds of suffering are being experienced by your brotherhood throughout the world. And after you have suffered a little while, the God of all grace, who has called you to his eternal glory in Christ, *will himself restore, confirm, strengthen, and establish you*" (1 Peter 5:8–10, emphasis added).
- "Put on the whole armor of God, *that you may be able to stand against the schemes of the devil.* For we do not wrestle against flesh and blood, but against the rulers,

against the authorities, against the cosmic powers over this present darkness, against the spiritual forces of evil in the heavenly places. Therefore take up the whole armor of God, *that you may be able to withstand in the evil day, and having done all, to stand firm. Stand therefore,* having fastened on the belt of truth, and having put on the breastplate of righteousness, and, as shoes for your feet, having put on the readiness given by the gospel of peace. In all circumstances take up the shield of faith, with which you can extinguish all the flaming darts of the evil one; and take the helmet of salvation, and the sword of the Spirit, which is the word of God, praying at all times in the Spirit, with all prayer and supplication" (Eph. 6:11–18, emphasis added).

- "Be watchful, *stand firm* in the faith, act like men, be strong" (1 Cor. 16:13, emphasis added).

Practically speaking, what do we do to "stand firm" in spiritual warfare? Once it becomes clear that something supernatural is going on, immediately go into prayer. Ask God to shield and guard you from Satan's attack. Request angelic protection and rebuke the Enemy—something like this:

Heavenly Father, please protect me. Please send Your angels to guard and shield me. Frustrate the plans of the Enemy and show Yourself mighty. To you, Satan and demons, I tell you, leave, in Jesus' name. You have no right to be here, and I stand on the firm promises of God that I am His servant, His child, and He is my King. In Jesus' name, amen.

One day when my youngest daughter was grappling with fear, I told her the pretend story of a little girl who was once afraid of everything. Finally one day she got really mad and said the same phrase every time someone tried to scare her. She said, "Not today, bully!" We'd all be a little healthier if we used that line. The next time the Enemy starts messing with your mind, worry begins to creep in, and the what-if scenarios start to fly, just say, "Not today, bully!" and hand the fight over to God in prayer. Trust He's going to take care of you. Decide today to take back your life from being pushed around by God's enemy.

CHAPTER 13

WHAT GOD CAN PRODUCE WITH OUR PAIN

*Don't run from tests and hardships, brothers
and sisters.* As difficult as they are, you will
ultimately *find joy in them; if you embrace them,
your faith will blossom under pressure.*
—James, writer and Jesus' brother[1]

Can we find anything good, anything redeemable, coming from our struggle with fear? Is it merely a trial, something we are to only endure or survive? Or could God be up to something in the midst of our chaos?

I believe not only that God can redeem our pain, but that He has already begun working.

God has promised us, His children, that He will redeem every trial we go through. Consider Romans 8:28, which says, "And we know that for those who love God all things work together for good, for those who are called according to his purpose."

Unfortunately, this verse is often misquoted and misinterpreted. While I might not be a New Testament scholar or a Greek linguist, I am quite certain about what it does *not* say: that everything is always good or that it comes down to a matter of perspective. This verse does not mean we have no right to be troubled because "it's all good."

Paul is saying God does not waste suffering and pain. For those who are called "His" (His children, His sheep, His body, His followers, His believers—that is, true Christians), He will redeem all situations for the greater glory and good plan that He has in place. Redemption means He will use, turn, change, bless, and buy our troubles back. There's no guarantee we will see the point, understand the purpose, or be assured through the circumstance; it means God knows what He's doing and can turn garbage into gold, trash into treasure. This gives value to our suffering. Though we suffer, God brings something good out of the situation. Our pain becomes a catalyst for blessing.

Even with my untrained, limited eyes, I have seen how God has used my personal challenges to make me more into the image of His Son, Jesus Christ, and bless those around me. I think He is doing the same with you.

I have found eight elements of redemption in our struggle with anxiety and fear. They have to do with enhancing our relationship with Christ, strengthening our relationships with others, and transforming our souls. From our jaded perspective, we might still deem our difficulties to be not "worth the pain," but we can either have pain by itself or have pain with redemptive elements.

Please join me as we look with a different set of lenses at our journey so we can see God's handiwork on the messy canvas of our lives. I would suggest highlighting or underlining each concept as you read to be able to refer back as needed for encouragement.

A CLOSER RELATIONSHIP WITH GOD

There is no greater remedy to our suffering than the power of drawing closer to our Creator. "Draw near to God, and he will draw near to you" (James 4:8). When no man can relieve us of our torment, we are forced to run to the only solution. My reality is that I cling to God with all I have, because I cannot live without Him. Would we know Him as well if we didn't struggle as we do? Would our prayer lives be as active? Would our desperation be as great? Would our adherence to His side be as tenacious?

I doubt it.

Desperation is a powerful motivator. I am living proof. Growing up a scared kid with no one who understood me and certainly no one who could fix my fear, I learned very early on that it was God or nothing. I quickly found that He was my only solace; He was my only peace. As much as I feared Him, I knew I could not live without Him. For that reason alone, I devoured Scripture. I prayed more than many young people pray. I pressed in to Him as tightly as I could. God and Christianity were no mere academic exercise for me. They were my hope and my life. A crucial reason I am a pastor today is that I have intimately seen the power of a personal relationship with God, who has walked this crazy life with me. I want everyone to have this same access to Him that I have experienced.

AN INCREASED LONGING FOR HEAVEN

A second blessing from my disorder is that it has made me long for heaven.

Paul wrote, "For to me to live is Christ, and to die is gain" (Phil. 1:21). As I reflect on my easygoing, laugh-filled, people-pleasing personality, I wonder whether I would long for heaven at all, as Paul did, without this condition. My only true reason for wanting heaven the way I do is that it's where my Jesus is. Other people have a motivation to go to heaven because they don't much like life on earth. Well, I like earth. I like the people down here. I like my home. I like my things. But the more I like my things here, the less I long for heaven. Without the pressure of my anxiety disorder, my contentedness on this planet could make me drive my tent stakes even deeper here and devalue heaven.

Ironically, I'm afraid of heaven because I've never been there before and because the Devil torments me with irrational fears of being rejected from entering. Yet that same fear propels me to want the Enemy quieted down once and for all, so I can finally be the peaceful man God designed me to be.

A GREATER DEPENDENCE ON GOD

The third redemptive element of suffering is making us entirely dependent on God. In modern-day American Christianity, we tend to celebrate autonomy and standing on our "own two feet." That is not the way of the Hebrew scriptures, nor the desire of God. He tells us in no uncertain terms that *we* exist because *He* exists. Jesus said:

> Abide in me, and I in you. As the branch cannot bear fruit by itself, unless it abides in the vine, neither can you, unless you abide in me. I am the vine; you are the branches. Whoever abides in me and I in him, he it is that bears much fruit, for apart from me you can do nothing. (John 15:4–5)

Jesus made it clear—apart from Him we can do nothing. This is true, because we were primarily created for two great purposes: bringing glory *to* God and having a relationship *with* God.

God *wants* us to be dependent on Him, even more than He desires us to *have to* be dependent on Him. The whole idea of proverbially saying, "Take the day off, God, I've got it from here" is repugnant to His heart. He did not make us to walk away from Him and live our own independent lives. He made us to be with Him, and our challenges require us to lean on Him more than we would otherwise.

Take a look at the following passages:

- "Trust in the LORD with all your heart, and do not lean on your own understanding. In all your ways acknowledge him, and he will make straight your paths. Be not wise in your own eyes; fear the LORD, and turn away from evil. It will be healing to your flesh and refreshment to your bones" (Prov. 3:5–8).

- "And he said to them, 'Follow me, and I will make you fishers of men.' Immediately they left their nets and followed him" (Matt. 4:19–20).
- "If we live by the Spirit, let us also keep in step with the Spirit" (Gal. 5:25).
- "Woe to those who go down to Egypt for help and rely on horses, who trust in chariots because they are many and in horsemen because they are very strong, but do not look to the Holy One of Israel or consult the LORD!" (Isa. 31:1).

You and I are compelled to be dependent on Him. We have no choice. We cannot make it on our own. Our bodies will not sustain us and our emotions will not hold us up. We need God to be able to survive day to day.

MORE HUMILITY

As Christians, we are to display many virtues in our lives. But for some reason humility is especially important to God. Being humble is the antithesis of being prideful. God draws the humble close to Him, while resisting the proud (James 4:6). Our blessing as we live in fear is being given a built-in "spiritual pacemaker" that shocks us when we get out of line. Arrogance is hard to pull off when you're scared of your own shadow. Being cocky is impossible when you need help every day.

For this reason I think it's appropriate to put some of our suffering into the category of "thorn in the flesh." Paul was given great insight and gifts from God. Jesus personally called him through a visible appearance (Acts 26:15–16; 1 Cor. 15:8). Through visions, he was taken up into heaven to see things he couldn't even write about (2 Cor. 12:2). He was spiritually gifted more than most people (1 Cor. 14:18). He was one of the greatest and most effective Christian evangelists the world has ever seen. The list goes on. But Paul's life wasn't perfect. Even beyond the terrible persecution he faced—beatings, stoning, and imprisonments (2 Cor. 11:23–27)—he was given what he called a "thorn in the flesh."

> To keep me from becoming conceited, I was given a thorn in my flesh, a messenger of Satan, to torment me. Three times I pleaded with the Lord to take it away from me. But he said to me, "My grace is sufficient for you, for my power is made perfect in weakness." Therefore I will boast all the more gladly about my weaknesses, so that Christ's power may rest on me. That is why, for Christ's sake, I delight in weaknesses, in insults, in hardships, in persecutions, in difficulties. For when I am weak, then I am strong. (2 Cor. 12:7–10 NIV)

No one knows for sure what Paul's thorn was—illness, poor eyesight, emotional torment—but I don't think knowing the specifics matters. The point is not *what* the thorn was, but what it *produced* in Paul's life and for what purpose he received it.

Look at the context of his words. Paul has just been writing about all the amazing things God had done with him and through him, and then he reveals that he has a dramatic struggle. He says he prayed three times for it to go away and

God said no. With clear direction, he was to bear that cross and roll with whatever it was. He trusted that God knew what He was doing.

Unlike Paul, I have not heard a clear no, so I am still praying about my situation. Thankfully, with some reflection I can see some of the things God has done and is doing with my own suffering. If Paul needed something to humble him, then who am I to think I don't? Truly, who among any of us, for that matter?

INCREASED COMPASSION, CONSIDERATION, AND CONNECTION

Suffering tends to produce depth of character. Much of the distance we try to create between ourselves and others is removed when we land flat on our backs at the foot of the cross.

> We rejoice in our sufferings, knowing that suffering produces endurance, and endurance produces character, and character produces hope, and hope does not put us to shame, because God's love has been poured into our hearts through the Holy Spirit who has been given to us. (Rom. 5:3–5)

Need is a connecting agent. Think of the bond between a baby and his or her mother. When we admit we have a need and reach out to others for help, they can be empowered and feel valued. When people reach out to us, our hearts can be attuned to their needs because of our own suffering. Praying for others is much easier when we recognize what their pain feels like. Instead of quickly judging them, we remember how we feel and how we want to be treated. In short, our suffering can help build community.

NEW OPPORTUNITIES FOR MINISTRY

If we are in a position of leadership or are influencers of people, many will assume we "have it all together" and our lives are easy and perfect. Sharing authentically about our journeys brings us down off that pedestal so we can be helpful role models and teachers. Consider Paul's words in 2 Corinthians:

> Blessed be the God and Father of our Lord Jesus Christ, the Father of mercies and God of all comfort, who comforts us in all our affliction, so that we may be able to comfort those who are in any affliction, with the comfort with which we ourselves are comforted by God. (2 Cor. 1:3–4)

My congregation knows I'm a messed-up, weak individual, just like they are. My weakness allows me to speak into their lives without them feeling judged or devalued. In the same way, the soccer mom down the street who is having problems in her marriage might not think she can open up to you, because your life seems picture perfect. But once she hears you, too, struggle in life, she might be more willing to be vulnerable and share her heart.

A PURIFIED FAITH

Despite how dysfunctional it is, sometimes we attempt to live moral and pure lives out of fear. If we believe in heaven and hell, God and the Devil, right and wrong, then we do not want to make God mad at us. We know that He is not going to be pleased about what we do against His will.

Unfortunately, this idea might drive some people to run away from God or anything religious. It can even lead to a fear of death, because dying brings us closer to God's judgment. As I mentioned, Satan has used this lie against me personally. Growing up I faced most of my days worrying that it would be my last, knowing I will come face-to-face with God and have to answer for what I've done.

Of course, this kind of thinking is irrational for true believers. The Bible clearly says Jesus Christ died for our sins and that we are not saved because of our righteous acts or our own purity, but solely on the merits of Jesus Christ's payment for our disobedience by His sinless life and death on the cross. According to the apostle Paul, "There is therefore now no condemnation for those who are in Christ Jesus" (Rom. 8:1). He went on to write,

> What then shall we say to these things? If God is for us, who can be against us? He who did not spare his own Son but gave him up for us all, how will he not also with him graciously give us all things? Who shall bring any charge against God's elect? It is God who justifies. Who is to condemn? Christ Jesus is the one who died—more than that, who was raised—who is at the right hand of God, who

indeed is interceding for us. Who shall separate us from the love of Christ? Shall tribulation, or distress, or persecution, or famine, or nakedness, or danger, or sword? As it is written, "For your sake we are being killed all the day long; we are regarded as sheep to be slaughtered." No, in all these things we are more than conquerors through him who loved us. For I am sure that neither death nor life, nor angels nor rulers, nor things present nor things to come, nor powers, nor height nor depth, nor anything else in all creation, will be able to separate us from the love of God in Christ Jesus our Lord. (vv. 31–39)

The redemptive part of this twisted conundrum—how Jesus has turned my self-condemnation into glory—is that I keep a much closer eye on how I live as a person who walks under the banner of Christ. For good or for bad, all kinds of alarm bells go off internally when I think about doing something outside God's will, which serves as a rather helpful deterrent against bad behavior. Because I value what God thinks of me and because I am hypersensitive to the thought of wrongdoing, I keep short accounts with God. I talk to Him day by day about what's happening in my life and continually confess where I am and what I'm doing. This type of constant connection is beneficial, and I hope to mature to the place where I do it more from my desire to be in a healthy relationship with God than from fear.

My faith is also purified when anxiety forces me to consider my motivations for why I believe. If I'm a Christian because I think it's going to make life easier, I'll never last. We all know true faith can make life tougher at times. I believe the test of whether I'm a true Christian is whether I can wholeheartedly agree with Job's line about God in Job 13:15: "Though he slay me, yet will I hope in him" (NIV). I believe this so much that I've made it one of my life verses.

If we love God for *what He provides*, then we will stop loving Him when He stops producing for us. It's the "What have you done for me lately?" syndrome. But if we love God because of *who He is*, then our love will endure. The torment of long-term anxiety constantly presses us to our limits, forcing us to ask, "Why do I love God? Why am I a Christian?" I am not a Christian because it works best for me. I am a Christian because Jesus is the only One who showed up and rescued me! He is my only hope. No other options are on the table. I love the Lord desperately for who He is and what He's already done for me eternally, beyond what He provides for me day to day.

God could have taken my anxiety away a long time ago, but He didn't—on purpose. That doesn't change my love or adoration for Him. God is good all the time, and I refuse to allow my circumstances to dictate my theology. Yes, I'm a mess, but that doesn't mean God isn't good, He doesn't care, or He is unable to change my situation. My anxiety drove the engine that powered the bit to drill down to the bedrock of that kind of faith, trust, and relationship, and I'm thankful for it.

BLESSINGS TO OTHERS

I'm sure you are quite aware that our anxiety is difficult for those around us. I'm thankful that God can use our pain to bless other people too. Sometimes God uses our difficulties as a chisel to shape the characters of the people we interact with the most. My wife, Suzi, would tell you she has grown tremendously through my struggle. This battle we have fought together has developed her understanding of suffering, her compassion for people with mental health issues, and her ability to be unselfish.

When I'm having a panic attack, I wreck Suzi's plans just as much as I wreck mine. Even though everything in her wants to get angry and walk away, she doesn't. Instead she is able to minister to and take care of me, and she grows. The woman I am married to today is even more wonderful than the woman I married in 1995. God has chiseled out her beauty in His image, and part of that process has been learning to live with someone who struggles.

Maybe you have someone in your life who is deeply affected by your bouts of anxiety. (Or maybe you are this person in someone's life and you're reading this book to better understand what's going on.) Know that God is working on others the same time He is working on you. The chisel God uses certainly never feels good when He is at work, but when the useless parts are stripped away we are much closer to being His beautiful masterpiece.

While we should always do everything we can to lighten the burdens on the ones we love, take heart that you are not a burden to those around you. Trust that God will redeem your pain so He is more glorified and the kingdom of God is advanced through you.

CHAPTER 14

THREE TRUTHS
TO TREASURE

The Kingdom of Heaven is like a treasure
that a man discovered hidden in a field.
—Jesus, Savior of the world[1]

I'm sorry you are hurting.

Has anyone said this to you recently? If not, let me repeat—I'm very, *very* sorry you are hurting.

I totally understand, and the pain I know you must feel breaks my heart. I wouldn't want this fear put on my worst enemy, so to know you are struggling makes me sad. I know somehow Jesus is redeeming all you are going through.

I'm proud of you for doing your best up to this point to live as healthfully and with as much integrity as you can, even though your life is very tough.

When I was young, my older sister was my best friend.

She would laugh with me, teach me, and, when she got older, take me on some of her dates. When I had drama of my own, she would see it in my eyes and ask me if I was okay. Usually I told her I was, although I'm afraid my countenance betrayed me. If someone had hurt me, she could see the words were still stinging. But then she would say this one line that I still hold on to: "Do you want me to break their legs?"

She didn't have to know who had hurt me or what the problem was. She wasn't even a member of the Mafia. She was just saying she loved me so much she was willing to stand up for me. She wanted to make things right.

I want very much to convey that same heart to you right now. If I could wish away your pain, I would. If I could "break the legs" of your anxiety, I would. Just know that you aren't alone. A lot of us are standing with you on this journey, and we really do care.

I have shared a lot of information with you—all of which I have used myself—and I hope you have found it not only insightful but practical. As we wrap up our journey together, I want to first challenge you one more time to make the healthiest changes you can. Second, I want to repeat and review three of the most powerful and important ideas I've shared.

1. Make healthy changes in the good times to be equipped for the bad times.

   Be wise about your choices. Don't merely thank the Lord for a respite from your anxiety but then not use the time to your advantage. Commit to taking back as much control of your mind and heart as you possibly can. Control the things you *can* control and adjust what you *can* adjust.

2. You are the master of your own mind—not the other way around.

   Your mind shouldn't have the freedom to wander anywhere it wants. You are in charge—not your passions, fears, worries, anxieties, or thoughts. You need to control your constant processing of what-if scenarios. Jesus said, "Don't be anxious about tomorrow. God will take care of your tomorrow too. Live one day at a time" (Matt. 6:34 TLB). We waste so much energy, time, and joy fearing what will never occur. Remind yourself of the countless times you worried about events that never happened and how much more you would have enjoyed that time had you only relaxed and taken things in stride. Apply that truth to today and tomorrow.

3. Watch your inputs.

   Be very careful what you let into your mind and input into your heart. If you were educated in the computer age, you might remember the phrase teachers would say: "Garbage in; garbage out." If you continually soak in things that trigger anxiety, you are going to struggle more. If you dwell on what will contribute toward your peace, you will reap the benefit. You might need to do a media fast to shut down scary, fear-inducing news stories or advertising that plays on your fears, or maybe avoid TV or movies that set you on edge. I have to avoid any TV hospital shows where kids get sick and might die. This is one of my triggers—threats to my own children's health.

   Be wise and think through what is entering your atmosphere. Proper control brings peace.

As your pastor—at least as you read this book—let me encourage you with three final truths. Let these soak in deep for real change.

GOD LOVES AND CARES FOR YOU

God is able to help you, and He has not left you abandoned and alone. I'm a fanatic about truthfulness and integrity in speech, so I wouldn't tell you these things if they were not true. I believe the Bible with all my heart, and the Word clearly expresses these truths for you.

God's Word says He loves us. The well-known Bible verses John 3:16–17 say:

> For God so loved the world, that he gave his only Son, that whoever believes in him should not perish but have eternal life. For God did not send his Son into the world to condemn the world, but in order that the world might be saved through him.

The Greek word for *world* used here is *kosmos* and generally means the part of the world systems that are anti-God. These verses mean God loved His creation so much that, even though they wanted to rebel, to be free of Him, to defy His rule, to ignore His reign, and to reject His presence, He still sent His Son, Jesus Christ, into the *kosmos* to make a way for them to be rescued.

The apostle Paul wrote:

For while we were still weak, at the right time Christ died for the ungodly. For one will scarcely die for a righteous person—though perhaps for a good person one would dare even to die—but God shows his love for us in that while we were still sinners, Christ died for us. Since, therefore, we have now been justified by his blood, much more shall we be saved by him from the wrath of God. For if while we were enemies we were reconciled to God by the death of his Son, much more, now that we are reconciled, shall we be saved by his life. More than that, we also rejoice in God through our Lord Jesus Christ, through whom we have now received reconciliation. (Rom. 5:6–11)

Even God's enemies—all who have sinned and turned away—have been given a way to be saved because of His incredible love, care, and concern for the human race (Luke 19:10).

Maybe you've been wondering how you can join into the family of God and receive all the blessings of a caring heavenly Father over you. Maybe you want this good news to be the defining factor of your life as well. It's strikingly unsophisticated and startlingly free. What the Bible calls the gospel—the "good news"—is simply this: Jesus Christ died for our sins (the bad stuff we've done and the distorted character we've become). He was buried in the tomb and was resurrected on the third day. He is alive today, calling all mankind back to Himself (1 Cor. 15:1–4).

How do we partake in this salvation? Paul tells us in Romans 10:9–13:

If you confess with your mouth that Jesus is Lord and believe in your heart that God raised him from the dead, you will be saved. For with the heart one believes and is justified, and with the mouth one confesses and is saved. For the Scripture says, "Everyone who believes in him will not be put to shame." For there is no distinction between Jew and Greek; for the same Lord is Lord of all, bestowing his riches on all who call on him. For "everyone who calls on the name of the Lord will be saved."

Because this gift is open for all to receive, God's incredible love is now demonstrated and made available to you. If you have trusted Christ by faith, all these beautiful truths of Scripture apply to you as His child.

You must first receive and accept that God loves you and cares for you. I realize that for most of us who live in fear, accepting this truth is easier said than done. Our insecurities can allow us to feel otherwise. Many days it's hard for me to believe as I look around at my circumstances, but it's still true.

God's love and care make Him intensely protective of us, and everything that happens in our lives is personal to Him. The Bible says His ears are attentive to the cries of His people. The great joy of what Christ did on the cross was that He gave us access to God and fixed the relationship that was broken. Once it is repaired, we have full access to engage with God personally, and we can do that knowing He has love waiting for us.

GOD IS IN CHARGE

We have talked about how God is big. Really big. But what we say we believe about Him and what we truly believe are sometimes different. We are often afraid and anxious because we don't truly believe God can solve our problems. If we truly trusted He was good, cared for us, and was able to do something about our situation, we would be far more peaceful.

The word we use for God's control over everything is *sovereignty*. This means nothing can happen without His knowledge and approval. Then comes the obvious question: "Why are bad things still happening?" The simple answer is that the human race said no to God and decided to do things their own way—and to this day still is. God allowed the consequences of that decision to take their full effect. But unwilling to leave us alone in our rebellion, He sent Jesus Christ to save us. He is currently intensifying His work, and one day He will return to clean up once and for all.

Until that time, bad things will happen to relatively good people. It's incredibly frustrating, and God doesn't like it either. This is not the way He designed life to be. But make no mistake—He's still in charge regardless of the choices we have made. Nothing exists that doesn't serve His plan in some capacity. This includes evil, the Devil, suffering, and death. When God is done with those things, He will put them away. Nothing is outside His scope of rule.

Our heavenly Dad is in charge, and because He loves us, we need not fear. There is no reason to worry that He doesn't see or care about our problems. Anything that happens to His kids is personal to Him. Likewise, there is no reason to think any problem is too big for Him to handle, because He is the Master of the universe.

Messes are not a problem for God. He is infinitely creative when it comes to fixing problems and taking care of His people. Let me remind you of the size and creativity of God's problem solving in the past: He wanted to make Abraham the father of the Jewish nation, which He promised would outnumber the sand of the seashore. The only problem was that Abraham didn't have any kids. He was already eighty-five years old, and his wife, Sarah, was seventy-five. In a panic, they concocted a plan for Abraham to bypass Sarah and have a child with another woman, lacking the faith to believe God could handle the situation. That didn't turn out very well, but our God kept moving forward with His plan. When Abraham was one hundred and Sarah was ninety, God miraculously provided that promised child, Isaac. Who would have thought all the ethnic and national Jews of the world would come from that one little boy?

When God wanted to raise up a deliverer for His Jewish people from Egypt, there was one barrier: Pharaoh was killing all the Hebrew baby boys. Did that stop God? Of course not. He had baby Moses put into a basket that floated down the river and was scooped up by Pharaoh's daughter, who raised him—even as he was nursed by his real mother. God orchestrated it so that Moses trained for forty years in Egypt's best universities and was driven into the desert to learn how to hear God and lead sheep. God then enabled Moses to return to lead His people to freedom. *Yeah, I wouldn't have thought of all that either!*

The New Testament has its share of these accounts too. God wanted to reach the Maltese people with the gospel, so He crashed Paul's ship on the island and had him bitten by a poisonous viper that didn't kill him. That amazed the villagers, who then took him to their leader's dad. Paul healed the man in the power of Jesus and was able to share the love of Christ with the whole island. *That's one way to evangelize a people!*

What about the miraculous angel release of Peter from prison or the visions that connected two totally different people like Paul and Cornelius? Good stuff.

If God can save people through the incarnation of Jesus Christ—taking on flesh and living among us, then suffering the cross only to die and come to life again in three days—I think He can handle our freak-outs. Don't you?

Whether it's natural or supernatural or a mixture, God can handle it. Whether it's silly or serious, He's got it. Whether it is "impossible" or doesn't matter, He can fix it. Please take comfort in that.

GOD HASN'T ABANDONED YOU

Some of us reason that if God is powerful and God is good, and yet we still suffer, then maybe He has forgotten about us, or maybe He set the world spinning and then walked away.

I know it feels that way, but nothing could be further from the truth.

- God is omnipresent, so where would He go? The psalmist said it this way: "Where shall I go from your

Spirit? Or where shall I flee from your presence? If I ascend to heaven, you are there! If I make my bed in Sheol, you are there! If I take the wings of the morning and dwell in the uttermost parts of the sea, even there your hand shall lead me, and your right hand shall hold me. If I say, 'Surely the darkness shall cover me, and the light about me be night,' even the darkness is not dark to you; the night is bright as the day, for darkness is as light with you" (Ps. 139:7–12).

- God promised to never leave or forsake us. "Be strong and courageous. Do not fear or be in dread of them, for it is the LORD your God who goes with you. He will not leave you or forsake you" (Deut. 31:6).

- When Sarah's unwanted handmaid Hagar was kicked out of the house to go and die with her son, Ishmael, God visited her and she called Him Beer-lahai-roi, which means "the God who sees and looks after me" (see Gen. 16:13–14).

- When Elisha's servant panicked at the size of the incoming enemy, Elisha prayed that the Lord would open his servant's eyes to the reality of the situation. When the young man looked around again, he saw the surrounding hills filled with heavenly horses and chariots of fire (2 Kings 6:15–17).

- Jesus healed a blind man who didn't see Him coming and didn't know who He was (John 9).

- Even when the disciples were straining to row their boat against the storm and were frustrated and scared, Jesus was watching them from the shore (Mark 6:45–52).

Maybe the most beautiful and poetic way God expresses His care over us is in the metaphor of a shepherd with his sheep. Both in Psalm 23 and John 10, we see God present Himself as a Good Shepherd. The Greek word in John 10:11–14 for *good* means "winsome, beautiful, lovely, attractive." This means He's not just capable, but He's the kind of shepherd who would make every lamb proud to be under his care. Through those passages, He expresses His love and care, explaining that even though things get dark ("Even though I walk through the valley of the shadow of death, I will fear no evil, for you are with me" [Ps. 23:4]), He is right there with us and can protect us from any evil that comes. I would encourage you to read those two passages over and over until they saturate your heart and you believe them with every fiber of your being.

God is watching over you. You are not alone. You are not forsaken or abandoned. He does care deeply about you and your situation. When you are tempted to ask why He doesn't help more or just fix your fear, remember that it's not the best scenario yet. Once it is, He will. Until then, we are to trust He is aware and knows exactly what He's doing.

—

As with any important idea, these three truths must be embraced not just cognitively but emotionally. This requires investing time into soaking them in. We would love to be able to hear something one time and have it register in our hearts for good, but that's never the case. Even a sponge needs a moment to soak up the water upon immersion.

If you are a visual learner, write them on index cards and

post them on the refrigerator, on the bathroom mirror, or on the dash of your car. For those with auditory learning styles, you might need to repeat them out loud periodically until they ring true. For those who are intellectual analyzers, maybe it would be helpful to do a full study through the Bible on each individual point. Somehow we need to be able to engage with all three of these concepts beyond merely reading them and waiting for change. How can you creatively allow the truth of these statements to enter into your soul? Whatever your answer, don't just think about it; put it into practice today.

Finally, I want to encourage you that just because you have suffered in the past or are suffering now doesn't mean you will always suffer. God might touch you with His healing hand, or your body might finally adjust, or you might find that one golden ticket way of managing your anxiety or pain. Don't give up hope, and don't walk this journey alone. So many of us know what you are going through and are partners with you in finding a solution. Keep searching, keep praying, and keep your chin up.

As we close, please do me a favor and write your own first name in the blanks below. Then allow me to pray for you by reading the prayer out loud with your name in place.

Dear heavenly Father, I pray that You would comfort _____. I pray that You would draw close and put Your healing hand upon _____. If it is within Your will, would You heal _____ in Jesus Christ's name? If You wish to demonstrate Your love to _____ through a struggle, please reveal Yourself and what You are doing so

_____ might rejoice in You. We believe You are good and You are loving. We believe the only way You would allow this to continue in our lives is for a greater purpose. We trust You. We love You. In the precious name of Jesus, amen.

ACKNOWLEDGMENTS

I wish to acknowledge some of the crucial people involved in this process to bring about God's best:

My editor and cowriter, Robert Nolan.

My sweet and brilliant agent, Lisa Jackson of Alive Communications.

My publisher and fellow creative, Joel Kneedler, the amazing staff at Thomas Nelson, (Meaghan Porter, Lori Cloud, Marissa Pellegrino, Kristi Smith, the promotions and editing team, and all of you who make me look good behind the scenes), and Jean Bloom.

Thank you for helping me transform this book into a tool for the kingdom of God that will love on as many as possible.

NOTES

Chapter 1: Why Me, Lord?

1. Amy Spencer, "Amanda Seyfried: The Most Down-to-Earth Member of the New Glam Guard," *Glamour*, April 2010, http://www.glamour.com/magazine/2010/03/amanda-seyfried-the-most-down-to-earth-member of the glam new guard.
2. *American Heritage® Dictionary of the English Language*, 5th ed., s.v. "phobia," http://www.thefreedictionary.com/phobia.

Chapter 2: The Agitating Angst of Adulthood

1. Tom Wilson, *Ziggyisms: Notable Quotes of Wisdom for Everyday Living* (Kansas City, MO: Andrews McNeel, 1997), 118–19.

Chapter 3: My Darkest Hour

1. Charles Haddon Spurgeon, *The Treasury of David*, vol. 1 (New York: I. K. Funk, 1882), 401.

Chapter 4: The Fear We Share

1. Jesse Singal, "A Q&A with Scott Stossel, Author of *My Age of Anxiety: Fear, Hope, Dread, and the Search for Peace of Mind*," *Daily Beast*, February 20, 2014, http://www.thedailybeast.com/articles/2014/02/20/a-q-a-with-scott-stossel-author-of-my-age-of-anxiety-fear-hope-dread-and-the-search-for-peace-of-mind.html.

2. The Kracken is a mythological beast of destruction, best known for his starring role in one of the Pirates of the Caribbean series of movies.

3. "Facts and Statistics," Anxiety and Depression Association of American, updated 2014, http://www.adaa.org/about-adaa/press-room/facts-statistics.

Chapter 5: Flying Through Fear: A Case Study

1. Walter Kirn, "What Gun Owners Really Want," *New Republic*, January 30, 2013, http://www.newrepublic.com/article/112194/walter-kirn-gun-owners.

Chapter 6: Meds: Magic or Mess?

1. Jim Murray, "Campbell Breaks Free Again," *Los Angeles Times*, August 15, 1991, http://articles.latimes.com/1991-08-15/sports/sp-633_1_earl-campbell.

2. Anita Soni, "Anxiety and Mood Disorders: Use and Expenditures for Adults 18 and Older, U.S. Civilian Noninstitutionalized Population, 2007," Medical Expenditure Panel Survey, December 2010, http://meps.ahrq.gov/data_files/publications/st303/stat303.pdf.

3. Jim Folk and Marilyn Folk, "Anxiety Effects on Society Statistics," AnxietyCentre.com, June 2015, http://www.anxietycentre.com/anxiety-statistics-information.shtml.

4. Ibid.

Chapter 7: From the Inside Out

1. Charles Darwin, *The Descent of Man* (1871; repr. New York: D. Appleton and Company, 1882), 123.

2. Mark Twain, "The Mysterious Stranger" in *The Mysterious Stranger and Other Stories* (New York: Dover, 1992), 117.

Chapter 8: From the Outside In

1. Gordon Smart, "Ellie: My Stepdad Was Horrible. He Had No Brains. If I Saw Him Again I'd Punch Him in the Face," *The Sun* (UK), http://www.thesun.co.uk/sol/homepage/showbiz /bizarre/3091719/Ellie-Goulding-on-her-turbulent-childhood .html?allComments=true.

Chapter 9: As It Is in Heaven

1. This statement has been attributed to Charles H. Spurgeon, Corrie ten Boom, and others.
2. C. S. Lewis, *The Complete C. S. Lewis Signature Classics* (San Francisco: HarperSanFrancisco, 2007), 116.

Chapter 10: Thy Will Be Done on Earth

1. Max Lucado, *Great Day Every Day: Navigating Life's Challenges with Promise and Purpose* (Nashville: Thomas Nelson, 2012), 80.

Chapter 11: The Three Lifesavers

1. Richard J. Foster, *Life with God: Reading the Bible for Spiritual Transformation* (New York: HarperOne, 2008), 135.

Chapter 12: Becoming a Battle-Ready Believer

1. Corrie ten Boom, *Defeated Enemies* (Fort Washington, PA: CLC Publications, 2012), 42.
2. C. S. Lewis, *The Screwtape Letters* (1942; repr. New York: HarperOne, 2001), ix.

Chapter 13: What God Can Produce with Our Pain

1. James 1:2–4 THE VOICE.

Chapter 14: Three Truths to Treasure

1. Matthew 13:44 NLT.

ABOUT THE AUTHOR

Lance Hahn is the senior pastor of Bridgeway Christian Church, host of the *Ask Pastor Lance* radio show, a conference speaker, an author, an adjunct professor, and the founder of LCH Ministries. He began teaching at Bridgeway Christian in 1997 in Rocklin, California, at the age of twenty-four, after four years of founding and pastoring an independent home church. Teaching God's Word in groups and preaching from the stage since the age of sixteen, Lance has developed an extraordinary ability to bring the Bible to life with passion and accuracy. He is known as both an expository and exegetical teacher, as well as a hilarious and fiery preacher. He takes God seriously, but not himself. He has been married to his beautiful wife, Suzi, since 1995, and they have two amazing daughters, Jillian and Andie. His downtime is spent pursuing his "nerdy" collecting hobbies and randomly trying new things. He is an animal lover at heart, and his dog Bella sleeps on his bed.